That Amazing Grace

2005

Other Titles by Dick B.

Dr. Bob's Library: Books for Twelve Step Growth

Anne Smith's Journal, 1933-1939: A.A.'s Principles of Success

Design for Living: The Oxford Group's Contribution to Early A.A.

The Akron Genesis of Alcoholics Anonymous

New Light on Alcoholism: The A.A. Legacy from Sam Shoemaker

The Books Early AAs Read for Spiritual Growth

Courage to Change (with Bill Pittman)

The Good Book and The Big Book: A.A.'s Roots in the Bible

That Amazing Grace

The Role of Clarence and
Grace S. in Alcoholics Anonymous

Dick B.

With a Foreword by Harold Hughes
Former U.S. Senator from, and Governor of, Iowa
Founder of S.O.A.R.

Paradise Research Publications
San Rafael, California

Paradise Research Publications, 247 Bret Harte Road, San Rafael, CA 94901

Cover Design: Richard Rose (Sun Lithographic Arts, Maui)

Publisher's Cataloging in Publication
(Prepared by Quality Books Inc.)

B., Dick.
  That amazing Grace : the role of Clarence and Grace S. in Alcoholics Anonymous / by Dick B.
with a foreword by Harold Hughes, former U.S. Senator from, and Governor of, Iowa; founder of S.O.A.R.
  p. cm.
  Includes bibliographical references and index.
  ISBN: 1-885803-06-0.
  1. S., Grace. 2. S., Clarence. 3. Alcoholics Anonymous--Biography. I. Title.
  HV5292.8.B34 1996   362.29'286'092
                         QBI96-20011

Library of Congress Catalog Card Number: 95-92858

If you don't stand for something, you will fall for almost anything.

Clarence S.

I only have one mission in A.A.—to lead as many kids as I can to the Lord.

Grace S.

And as you go, preach, saying, The kingdom of heaven is at hand. Heal the sick, cleanse the lepers, raise the dead, cast out devils: freely ye have received, freely give.

Matthew 10:7-8

Contents

Contents   ix

Foreword

It is important that everyone know their roots. It is important that the information be as simple and uncomplicated as it can be. Especially for those of us yearning to know the basis and truth of what we have been told is the only way we can live our lives. It is important that the source of our information be as well researched and expressed as is humanly possible. The author "Dick B." has done that in his many titles. I find this one to be another piece of the spiritual history that is needed to flesh out the body of knowledge surrounding this 20th Century spiritual awakening.

It has always been a matter of interest to me that, in this 20th Century, God chose to reveal more clearly to the lepers of our age, "the alcoholics," the message *He* had delivered centuries before. He selected unlikely messengers to say to us, "Forsake all things and follow in these footsteps, and I will give you life." When two or three gathered together and believed, the healing power of the universe reached to the very gates of hell saying in a very clear voice, "This is the way!"

It is reported that the author of our Declaration of Independence stated that the actual words of Jesus stood out in the Scriptures like diamonds in a dunghill. The healing words of the Good Book, that are the foundation of the words in the Big Book, also stand out like diamonds in a dunghill. The Founding Fathers (Apostles) of A.A. walked different paths, as did the disciples of Jesus centuries ago. They had differences, arguments, and confrontations. Is it any wonder that there are differences in A.A. today and were differences in early A.A.?

The vast majority of persons seeking to enter the gate leading to the road to freedom from addiction to alcohol are Christian in heritage. To them, to speak of God is to speak of Jesus of Nazareth. I do not hesitate to speak of my understanding of God openly; and this means I speak of my faith in Jesus openly. For the more than forty years I have labored with alcoholics, and the sixty years since I took my first drink—almost at the same time Bill and Dr. Bob met for the first time—I have never hesitated to use my full name while discussing my own confrontations with alcohol. Everyone knew me when I was drunk, and I am proud for everyone to know I have recovered. I have never found it to be a personal handicap for me, though I can well understand how it can be for others. I believe that to speak of one's own alcoholism using his or her own full name is a judgment call to be made by each individual. Using my full name publicly has resulted in reaching people beyond number with information as to how to get help.

The example of Clarence and Grace, as told by the author, leads me to believe that our Lord has blessed and honored their faith and their openness. I myself have received a blessing by reading these words as I hope you will also.

HAROLD E. HUGHES

Harold E. Hughes is the former Governor of, and United States Senator from, Iowa, and is the founder of SOAR.

Preface

This work marks a departure from the previous eight titles I have had published. The others explored and analyzed various components of the history of early A.A.'s spiritual roots and successes. My first title reviewed the books Dr. Bob studied and recommended. The second reported on the specifics Dr. Bob's wife Anne wrote and shared from the Bible, Christian literature, and the Oxford Group meetings with early AAs and their families. The third contained a comprehensive study of the Oxford Group's origins and impact on A.A. The fourth showed how it all came together at A.A.'s birthplace in Akron, Ohio. Two more examined the role the Reverend Sam Shoemaker played in inspiring and teaching spiritual ideas to Bill Wilson and other AAs. The next was a bibliography listing all the religious literature early AAs read for spiritual growth. And the last of this group examined in detail A.A.'s roots in the Bible.

Many of these have now been revised. Copies can now be found in archives and libraries and in the hands of A.A. delegates, volunteers, historians, and opinion molders. And we hope they will help AAs today both to understand the language of their steps and literature and to use the historical materials to achieve the same kind of spiritual growth and success early AAs attained, particularly in Ohio.

The success rate in early A.A. was astonishing. The Big Book claimed seventy-five percent of those who really tried were able to recover. Bill Wilson once claimed eighty percent. A survey of early Cleveland A.A. indicated ninety-five percent were succeeding. And Jack Alexander reported in his March, 1, 1941, *Saturday Evening Post* article that one-hundred-percent effectiveness with non-psychotic drinkers who sincerely wanted to quit was claimed by the workers of Alcoholics Anonymous.

Take your choice. But you cannot escape concluding that something was going on in early A.A. that is not going on in today's A.A. Fellowship.

It's my thesis that there is nothing which occurred in early A.A. that cannot be reproduced today among those who wish to learn and apply the early principles. Yet many have said to me directly that A.A. left the Bible and the Bible thumpers behind in Akron. Hence I have had these questions: Is there no longer any interest in the techniques and fellowship successes of early A.A. when Dr. Bob was using the Bible to help people learn about God, His power, His love, and His Will? Is there no longer any interest in what Anne Smith (Dr. Bob's wife) taught early AAs and their families and which seems to have produced much of our Big Book material and Step language? Is there no value in understanding the recovery structure which was so clearly and simply laid out by the Oxford Group and Sam Shoemaker?

Then came my acquaintance with Grace S. I had known very little about either Clarence or Grace S. But I recently spent a week in Minnesota and Wisconsin sharing the platform with Grace at various meetings and at a spiritual retreat. I saw that belief in God, in the accuracy and integrity of the Bible, and in the moral and spiritual principles of early A.A. was very much alive.

Clarence S. was one of the early pioneers who was present and active when A.A. was developing and succeeding remarkably well. Clarence later used the Bible, the Big Book, the Twelve Steps, and the principles of the Oxford Group to help thousands to recover. Clarence was unabashed in his mention of these spiritual tools. He founded spiritual retreats in A.A. which were highly successful, are still being held, and are growing in number and popularity. At these retreats, the Bible is freely discussed. Jesus Christ is frequently mentioned. Prayer and healing are commonplace.

Precise guidance for taking the Twelve Steps is part and parcel of the retreats. And there is immense enthusiasm.

I know, for I was there.

Clarence and Grace shared a mission and ministry. They worked closely together to sponsor people in their A.A. recoveries, to bring them to Christ, and to teach them from the Good Book and the Big Book how to live their sober lives successfully. Grace carries on to this day. And I've met the people who have been blessed by the continuing love, service, and witnessing that came from these roots in early A.A.

This title is, as I said, a departure. It contains a brief biography of Clarence and Grace. I've not done that before; and I am not doing it to publicize or eulogize two A.A. personalities. I am doing it to let people see that the principles of early A.A. are alive and well today among those courageous enough to espouse and apply them. This work is an historical account of recovery and deliverance that have been made available to AAs today through the beliefs and guidance of two dedicated, veteran AAs. It is a challenge to those who want to tread a similar path and need the courage and the proof to take a stand, recover, and grow spiritually.

The work is not an appeal to join Grace and her retreats. It will stand, I hope, as evidence that her love and courage can be an example to others. Grace is a living repository of our spiritual history. She specifically set out to learn it from Clarence. She speaks of it. She utilizes it. So did her late husband, Clarence. And so, I find, do a good many others who are now hungry for more knowledge of our spiritual roots and the reasons for our early successes. I've seen the hunger and enthusiasm in California, in Connecticut, in Vermont, in Florida, and in Hawaii among people who have scarcely heard of Clarence and Grace.

These other AAs are applying principles from the Bible, the Big Book, the Steps, and A.A. history that Clarence and Grace applied with great success. Their efforts are producing a success that parallels that in early A.A. And this title may help them and others to know they are not alone.

Acknowledgements

My son Ken again joined me at the bookshelves, the computer, the printer, and the editorial desk to make this work possible. I've mentioned his invaluable inspiration and assistance before. I've mentioned his skill as a Bible scholar. And I've mentioned his increasing knowledge of how to help drunks with their spiritual pursuits. In this current title, Ken joined me in Florida where we worked closely with Grace for more than a week to gather her recollections and records of what happened and happens in the ministry of Clarence and Grace S.

There have been direct assists from others connected with the ministry of Clarence and Grace. Clarence entrusted all his papers and archival material to Mitch K. of New York who has been studying and writing on that material for at least a decade. Several years ago, I spent substantial time with Mitch at an archives conference in West Virginia and then at a meeting in Connecticut. And Mitch was the first to acquaint me with Clarence's approaches to the A.A. recovery program. In my specific research for this book on Grace and Clarence, I must credit the following for substantial assistance in assembling the story: Grace herself, Steve and Sue F. in Florida, Ray G. at Dr. Bob's Home in Ohio, Susie H. in Minnesota, Ray M. in Hawaii, Dale and Carol M. in Wisconsin, Jack R. in Florida, John S. in Wisconsin, Dick S. in Florida, Danny W. in California, Berry W. in Idaho, and others who told me what Clarence and Grace stood for and accomplished.

My acknowledgements of other sources are amply covered and in much detail in my previous titles; but I'll mention those here whose contribution figured heavily in my research for this particular book—even though their contributions often preceded its preparation by some time.

Among the founding families: Sue Smith Windows and Betty and Bob Smith; John Seiberling, Dorothy Seiberling, and Mary Seiberling Huhn; Dorothy Williams Culver; Sally Shoemaker Robinson and Nickie Shoemaker Haggart.

Among Oxford Group people in America—Reverend Harry Almond, Mrs. W. Irving Harris, James Houck, T. Willard Hunter, James D. and Eleanor F. Newton, Richard Ruffin, L. Parks Shipley, Sr., and George Vondermuhll, Jr.; and abroad—Kenneth Belden, Sydney Cook, Michael Hutchinson, R. Mowat, and Garth Lean.

Then a host of AAs and A.A. historians including: Mel B., Dennis C., Ray G., Earl H., Gail L., Paul L., Frank M., Bob P., George T., Nell Wing, and Dr. Ernest Kurtz. Among my own group of A.A. sponsees and Bible fellowship members on Maui, I must mention Craig, Jeff, Matt, Shane, Nathanael, Ben, Bob, Chuck, Cody, Katy, Mike and Sharon, and others in the wings who are proving that the early A.A. program works today. And they have joined in helping me with various facets of my research and distribution. Nathanael was of particular help in working with me on the Internet—transmitting comments, letters, and drafts. Thanks too to my daughter-in-law Cindy and my A.A. sponsor, Henry B.

Special words of appreciation to Dr. Paul Wood, the Rev. Dr. Richard McCandless, Mrs. Walter Shipley, Leonard Firestone, Raymond Firestone (deceased), Martha Baker, Bob Koch and friends, R. Brinkley Smithers (deceased), the Thomas Pike Foundation, Doug Chambers, and Charles P. Mau.

Part 1

Getting Acquainted
with Grace and Clarence

1

My Introduction to Grace

You might say that even *meeting* Grace was a surprise.

I had been told she was almost eighty. She had undergone five bypass operations. One of her A.A. sponsees had led me to believe she was very frail and soon "going home to Jesus," as he put it. So there she was—at the Twin Cities Airport. Last off the plane—the porter pushing her toward us in a wheelchair.

But that's where her reported limitations ended, and the action began. Grace was, and is, a very beautiful lady. She was soft-spoken and had a Southern accent. She was attractively dressed. She was clearly interested in the vigorous five days of activities that lay ahead. And she was *ready to roll.*

I knew very little about her. I had heard that her late husband—A.A.'s venerable Clarence S.—had called her "Amazing Grace." The son of A.A.'s co-founder Dr. Bob had previously told me that Grace was conducting A.A. spiritual retreats in various parts of the United States—retreats that had originated with her husband Clarence before he died. I had learned from others that Grace was a committed Christian and a recovered alcoholic, active in A.A. I had spoken to her by phone from Hawaii at her home in Ponte Vedra Beach in Florida; and that was about all I knew.

I didn't know much about Clarence either. But I had *heard* several things about him. He was "controversial" in A.A., I had been told. He was "abrasive," one A.A. historian had written. He had frequently ignored A.A.'s "anonymity" tradition and unhesitatingly used his full name in identifying himself at the level of press and film. He had, others said, been very unhappy with many things A.A.'s co-founder Bill Wilson did in A.A.'s later years. And Clarence had often described *himself* as the "founder" of Alcoholics Anonymous.

And yet . . . I had personally met or listened to several admiring AAs whom Clarence had sponsored or "grand-sponsored" over the years. These men had maintained long-term sobriety in A.A. Furthermore, Clarence himself had claimed at the time of his death to have more sober time than anyone alive. He had been one of A.A.'s first forty "pioneers." Dr. Bob's daughter Sue had told me that Clarence "was all for Dr. Bob"—a real supporter of A.A.'s Akron co-founder. I had heard from several Roman Catholics in A.A. that they believed there would be no Roman Catholics in A.A. today but for Clarence's vigorous stand on behalf of those of that faith in 1939. And I had read that, through Clarence's zeal, A.A. had grown in one year from one group to thirty in Cleveland in the early days. Also, several of Clarence's sponsees had told me that Clarence—like Dr. Bob—had been a dedicated Christian.

And I had been busy for five years researching and writing about early A.A.'s biblical, Christian roots.

With that, one of Clarence's A.A. sponsees phoned me in Hawaii in early 1995. His name was Dale. He had read one of my latest books on the history of early A.A.'s spiritual roots and successes. Dale asked me to come to Amery, Wisconsin, and speak at an A.A. spiritual retreat. My topic was to be early A.A.'s spiritual history. Dale told me he had been sober some thirty years, that Clarence had been his sponsor, and that Clarence's widow Grace would be sharing at the program with me. Dale wanted to know if I would come.

Maui is a long way from Amery, Wisconsin; but I realized there was much to be learned from meeting Grace and exploring early A.A. history through her recollections. Grace was almost eighty, and time to meet and interview her was growing short. So

I was looking forward to the trip. But I short-changed myself in expectations. I never thought I would find what I found on meeting the "Amazing" Grace S. And the six days I spent with her in September of 1995 changed my whole outlook on today's A.A. and the potential for large-percentage recovery within its rooms.

Dale and I met Grace at the Twin Cities Airport in the Fall of 1995. Grace, Dale, several others, and I went to a small A.A. meeting that evening in Minnesota where the Chair had asked me to speak. Just prior to my departure from Maui, I had been delivered by prayer from persistent, excruciating back pain which had put my Wisconsin trip in jeopardy. That painful experience was fresh in my mind as all of us sat together just prior to the A.A. meeting. A young AA (Jim) walked into the meeting wincing with obvious pain. "What's the matter, Jim," another AA said. Jim replied that he was having severe back pains; and I could relate. But I probably would have sailed on with the meeting, had a moment of compassion for the young man, and then pushed his problem from my mind.

Not Grace! Just before the meeting began, she quietly approached the young man and asked him if he would like her to pray for him. Somewhat astonished, Jim replied, "Yes." And Grace then invited Dale to join her, lay hands on the man, and (silently) pray for him. That was immediately prior to an *A.A.* meeting! And the experience reminded me of what I had heard about early A.A. For early AAs—particularly Dr. Bob—had often prayed for people in their Fellowship.

The next night, Grace and I spoke at an enthusiastic Overcomers Outreach meeting. There was prayer by the leaders and speakers *before* the meeting. And Grace and I both joined in the prayers. There was a fine young male singer who gave a beautiful solo. Then Grace—who spoke first—delivered a wallop about the necessity for choosing which way one would go as he or she departed this world. Only to state graciously that she was going to defer to a much more important speaker who would tell the audience about A.A.'s spiritual roots. She said she could hear Clarence talking to her about early A.A. through the language in the next speaker's books—*my* books. And that was some introduction!

As the hours progressed in Wisconsin, I began asking Grace about Clarence. I soon realized there was much to be learned about this man, his knowledge of early A.A., his deep belief in the Bible, and the ministry he and Grace had conducted in taking new AAs through the Twelve Steps and "bringing them to the Lord"—as she and Clarence often put it.

Then the spiritual retreat commenced.

I watched Grace take suffering A.A. newcomers aside, kneel with them in a quiet place, and bring them to a surrender to God. Talks on recovery from alcoholism and A.A.'s Twelve Steps were a part of the scene. And then, on Saturday night, I addressed an attentive group on the history of early A.A.'s spiritual ideas.

Sunday morning, Grace was scheduled to be the featured speaker. But a mishap occurred. Dale's wife Carol was to have opened the meeting, but she was stricken with intense pain. Grace immediately helped arrange for a substitute Chair. Grace called several of us to a separate room before the meeting began. And each of us, in his or her own way, prayed for Carol's deliverance. One AA anointed Carol with oil. (For further reference, the reader may see the healing ministry described in James 5:14-15). Grace said to me, before she began, "Dick, I'll open the prayers, and you close." She did, and I did.

I have never, in all my A.A. years, seen such faith, fervor, and firm resolve as to the efficacy God's power among members of Alcoholics Anonymous. We all prayed. Dale took Carol to the doctor to be checked out. Grace spoke at the program. Word came to us that Carol was doing well. And Carol was back on deck in little over an hour.

Grace did not let up. She found a young man who was early in sobriety and absolutely terrified about a host of legal difficulties. She talked to him, prayed with him, and then asked me to work with the young man and see if I could help him in his legal approach, his Step approach, and his prayer approach. As she did so, I was returning in my mind to my own terror-filled early days of sobriety in A.A. and the legal entanglements that then lay before me. I therefore spent the bulk of the final retreat afternoon trying to help that young man.

And that is the way those September retreat days in cold Wisconsin passed by. Trusting in God. Asking for guidance. Praying for deliverance. And doing so within the framework of A.A.'s Big Book, Twelve Steps, and what some have called A.A.'s "Big, Big Book." I later found that Clarence also often referred to the Bible as A.A.'s "Big, Big Book."

Now just who *was* this Grace?

In a moment, we will take a brief look at her background. Then we will get on with some history about Clarence, Grace's recollections of him, and Clarence's accounts to her about A.A. and spiritual matters. We will also examine their dedicated ministry together, what Grace is doing to this very day, and how all this rich history can and does impact on others.

Will we talk about things that some AAs might not agree with? We surely will. Clarence did just that during all of his forty-six years of sobriety as he helped shape Alcoholics Anonymous and bring thousands of AAs to long-term sobriety within A.A.'s own rooms.

That is history. And it has everything to do with the seventy-five percent success rate early AAs were achieving in their formative years in Akron and the ninety-five percent success rate they achieved during Clarence's early work with AAs in Cleveland.

The surprise for me was that I found my much-sought-after history being applied in Amery, Wisconsin. I found that application in the person of, and the bold, courageous, unashamed, and successful ministry of, the seventy-eight year old widow of that "controversial" A.A. pioneer Clarence S.

2

"Amazing" Grace—A Biographical Sketch

Grace was born on December 26, 1916, at Cameron, in Lee County, North Carolina.

Her father, Marshall, came from English and Welsh stock. Her father's family had been of Methodist persuasion. Grace's mother, Bessie, was of Scottish descent and came from a Presbyterian family. As Grace puts it:

> My mother came to the Lord at the Cameron Baptist Church, and apparently she was a very different person after she had walked down the aisle in response to the altar call. This event occurred in 1906; and, many years later, my mother told me what had happened. She said "she had wanted to give her heart to Jesus Christ and had asked Jesus to be the Lord of her life." She said she had then run all the way to her godmother's house (a Mrs. Spivey)—"shouting all the way that she had given her life to Jesus."

Grace's father, Marshall, had, shortly thereafter, also gone down to the altar. Then Marshall and Bessie were married in the Cameron Baptist Church where all of their children were reared.

Grace was one of eleven children born to Marshall and Bessie; and Grace and her siblings all attended Sunday school at the Baptist Church in Cameron. Grace was introduced to the Bible at the earliest possible point in her life. Her mother read the Bible to the family every day and mostly from the New Testament. If a storm was gathering, Bessie would gather all the kids together, read from Psalms and Proverbs, and teach the children not to be afraid because, Grace said, "Mother said, 'Jesus is always with us.'"

When Grace entered high school, she acquired a Bible which she recalls as *Thompson's Chain Reference Bible*. She studied it every day. She continues her Bible study almost every day to the date of this writing and uses a King James Version. Virtually every line of her Bible is underlined; and most lines are highlighted with orange, pink, green, blue, or other colored markings. When Grace was "baptized with the Holy Spirit," she also began reading *The Living Bible Paraphrased*. Her copy is thoroughly underlined and annotated with her studies and with cross-references. Grace's King James Version contains a well-marked and highlighted Bible commentary at the end of it, as well as an equally well-marked portion titled "How to Study the Bible"—containing a day-to-day, twelve-month plan for Bible study.

Grace attended public schools at Cameron, North Carolina, where she completed high school. She then attended the University of Georgia at Athens, Georgia. In 1939, she went to work for Potomac Bell Telephone where she provided weather reports for all of the Armed Services during the initial period of World War II.

Grace married Herb M. on October 30, 1942. Herb was twenty-nine, and Grace was twenty-six. Herb had a son by a previous marriage. The mother had died as the result of an appendectomy when the son, Herb, Jr., was just an infant. Grace adopted Herb, Jr., on Mothers' Day of 1943. The son has always been known by the name "Duke;" and Grace currently lives with Duke and his family in Ponte Vedra Beach, Florida.

Shortly after their marriage, Grace and Herb, Sr., moved to Oklahoma City where Grace worked with her husband at "Herb's Supermarket" for about ten years. The pair then moved to Atlanta, Georgia, where they worked together in a business known as

Southern Stainless Steel. They worked there until 1967 at which time they moved to Florida to retire. Herb died on March 4, 1968. Meanwhile, Grace had succumbed to alcoholism. She was a periodic alcoholic. She believes she "crossed the invisible line" about 1963. But on the day of Herb's death, Grace had a rude awakening. She had been hospitalized, and her doctor came to her room in the morning and said that he had two things to tell her: first, that her husband had just died of a heart attack; second, that she was an alcoholic.

The doctor recommended A.A. And Grace recalls the unusual and loving way in which the A.A. alternative was suggested to her. Grace said to the doctor, "My God, I'm an alcoholic, what do I do?" He replied, "A.A. has the answer to all your problems." He asked her if she wished for some women AAs to visit her. Grace replied that he was the doctor, and that she would follow his advice. Then she asked, "How did you get all of this information about A.A.?" The doctor answered, "I've been sober three-and-a-half years in A.A." Grace said, "You need to tell me where an A.A. meeting is; and the moment you let me out of this hospital, I won't walk—I'll run to an A.A. meeting."

Grace was a thoroughly-churched lady.

When she was eight or nine, her sister Claire drove Grace and two sisters in a Model T to a Mr. Thomas's tobacco barn on the outskirts of Cameron. "Holiness" preachers came through town each time the tobacco crops were in. The preachers would pitch tents "just like Oral Roberts did." Grace recalls that there was a revival meeting every night which was attended by "poor white people and blacks" (the blacks not being permitted to attend white Protestant churches). Grace described the meeting she had attended clandestinely as a "holiness experience." The preachers taught the word of God. They opened the meeting up and "sang and sang and sang and danced and worshipped the Lord." Grace had been taught that such behavior was not appropriate, that one should reverence the Church and reverence God, but not mix the two. At the Holiness meeting, Grace heard those present speak in tongues, and there were "prophetic outpourings." But Grace was forbidden by her parents to attend further meetings of that nature.

When Grace was ten, she attended a revival meeting after the regular Cameron Baptist Church's services. She answered an altar call and told the minister, "I want to give my life to Jesus and live for him." She then received a water baptism and continued regular attendance at that church throughout high school. She also attended Southern Baptist churches in Athens, Georgia, and in Washington, D. C., and was married to Herb in a Baptist church in Washington, D. C.

When Grace and Herb moved to Atlanta in 1951, she and Herb joined a Methodist church of which they remained members until they moved to Jacksonville, Florida, in 1967. Shortly after Herb's death in 1968, Grace went to work as a "campus working director" at Flynn College in St. Petersburg, Florida. Grace worked at Flynn College until she married Clarence.

Grace met Clarence S. when she was fifteen months sober. In the Spring of 1969, Clarence had been invited to do the mortgage burning for the Penman Road Group (of A.A.) at Jacksonville Beach in Florida. The ceremony was to occur in July of 1969. A local A.A. "guru" asked Grace if she would like to have dinner with the "oldest living man in the world in A.A." Grace translated this to mean that Clarence at that time had been sober in A.A. longer than any other living member. (Actually, the guru was in error, for A.A.'s co-founder Bill Wilson was still alive; had, of course, been sober longer than any other A.A.; and was therefore the AA with the most sober time.)

Grace remembers well her first date with Clarence. She was driven by a friend to meet Clarence at the Holiday Inn at Jacksonville Beach. When she and the friend arrived at the hotel, Clarence was waiting in front. The friend said, "That's Clarence." Having been promised "the oldest living man," Grace was expecting a wheelchair, canes, or crutches. Hence, she exclaimed, "Clarence, come over here and give me a kiss." She wanted "to see if he was real." Clarence accommodated her, and off they went to a surf and turf dinner at Ninety By The Sea restaurant.

Dinner was ordered; and while the group was waiting, Clarence asked Grace to dance. Grace quickly learned, said, and later heard others say Clarence was "the world's best waltzer." After several dances and dinner, Grace and Clarence returned to the dance floor and continued in bliss until about two a.m. At that point, the pair left the floor. But Clarence said, "One more dance."

When they approached the floor, Clarence said, "I have something to tell you, but I don't quite know how to do it." Grace replied, "Well why don't you just tell me, and we'll go from there." Whereupon, the six-foot-tall Clarence grasped the chin of the five-foot-two Grace and said, "Grace, you're going to spend the rest of your life with me." Grace thought to herself, "Had he drunk too long or had he been sober too long."

Twenty-six months later, Clarence and Grace were married at the First Methodist Church in Atlanta, Georgia, on September 26, 1972. Clarence's son Dick (his only child, and by a prior marriage) was his father's best man. Grace's only son "Duke" gave Grace away. And, as Clarence had predicted, remain with Clarence for the rest of his life is exactly what Grace did.

3

Now about Clarence . . .

Most of Clarence's story can be heard on tapes or has been heard at the hundreds of meetings he addressed. It can also be read (in part) in his story "Home Brewmeister" in the personal narrative section of A.A.'s Big Book. Grace was neither acquainted nor present with Clarence during his earlier years. So we will here give only a few brief facts and leave to others the telling of Clarence's many stories about his family life and drinking career.

Clarence was born on December 26, 1902, in Cleveland, Ohio. He was the youngest of three brothers. Clarence attended East High School in Cleveland until his father died. Clarence was fourteen. At that time, in his third year, his mother made him quit school and go to work. He received some substantial additional education as the tutor for the blind child of a wealthy Cleveland family. That job permitted him to visit many art museums, operas, ballets, and plays in the company of the blind child. He also took special night courses at Cleveland College and Fenn College for three years in Cleveland, studying economics, business, credits, and collections.

Clarence's religious background was quite substantial.

Though his mother and father never took him to church, they sent him to a Protestant Sunday school with neighbors. Later, Clarence was involved in Bible study, prayer, meditation, and religious reading as a member of the Oxford Group (also known as "A First Century Christian Fellowship") during the time A.A. was an integral part of the Oxford Group. At this same time, he was receiving a good deal of Bible instruction directly from Dr. Bob's wife, Anne. Still later, Clarence attended one of Glenn Clark's famous religious convocations at Camp Farthest Out—an experience in which A.A.'s co-founder Dr. Bob and his wife Anne had also been involved.

Clarence was born again at the home of T. Henry Williams in Akron, Ohio; and the regularity of born-again experiences among the early AAs has also been confirmed to the author by A.A. oldtimer Larry B. of Cleveland, Ohio. (For details, see Dick B., *The Akron Genesis of Alcoholics Anonymous*, pp. 196-97). And, from his earliest A.A. days to the date of his death, Clarence continued his Oxford Group practices of Bible study, quiet time (which included prayer and meditation), the daily reading of Bible devotionals, and the reading of other Christian literature.

Clarence's first wife was named Dorothy; and there was a son, Dick, the issue of that marriage. Clarence worked for the City National Bank in Cleveland until he was fired for alcoholism at about age thirty-two. Clarence and Dorothy were divorced before Clarence was drafted into the Armed Services in World War II. Dorothy and the son Dick moved to California, and Clarence married a second wife, Selma.

By this time, Clarence had become sober and active in A.A. Selma's father was the director of Deaconess Hospital in Cleveland where Selma worked. Clarence frequently brought drunks to Deaconess Hospital to help them sober up. Selma's father and six brothers were ministers. Clarence and Selma moved to St. Petersburg, Florida. There Clarence served for three years as an Elder and President of the Trinity Evangelical and Reformed Church. Clarence and Selma belonged to the Trinity E and R Church in St. Petersburg for at least fifteen years; and Clarence helped raise most of the funds for the erection of the church, mortgage free, on land it had purchased in an orange grove.

Clarence's marriage to Selma ended in a divorce; but his religious life became even more intense.

Within six months after Clarence married his third wife Grace in 1971, Clarence joined Grace as a member of the Calvary Assembly of God Church which was located in Winter Park, Florida. We will have more to say about their activity in the Assemblies of God denomination when we speak of their mission and ministry. Suffice it to say at this point that they were devoted members of that denomination, that Clarence was baptized in the Holy Spirit in that church, that he received a water baptism at that time, and that he "received his prayer language" (i.e., he spoke in tongues).

Clarence and Grace owned a home at 142 S. Lake Triplet Drive in Casselberry, Florida. They lived there until Clarence's death on March 22, 1984.

In 1979, Clarence's sponsee Steve F. nominated Clarence to receive the prestigious Jefferson Award for Outstanding Public Service Benefitting Local Communities. Clarence first learned about his nomination from a radio station in Orlando, Florida. He asked Grace what she knew about it. Grace said, "Steve F. broached the idea to me, and said he wanted to submit your name for the local Jefferson Award, and I thought it would be great." Grace said, "I didn't know it was a thing that went up to other levels, and Clarence didn't either." Clarence came home that day with the local award.

Grace said:

We were in the Grand Cayman Islands doing A.A. The Associated Press called. I answered the telephone. The man asked me for Clarence, who was not available for the telephone. He told me Clarence had been selected for the award in his category at the state level. He told me to get in touch with a woman at the T.V. station. When we returned to Casselberry, Clarence got in touch with the woman as he was instructed. She told Clarence he was going to receive the Jefferson Award in Washington, D.C., at the United States Supreme Court.

Steve (Clarence's sponsee), his wife, and two children had been invited to go with us to Washington, D.C., for the award. Steve said to Clarence, "How much of a donnybrook do you

think this is going to stir up?" Clarence replied, "I don't think
there should be any. I've never had any anonymity. If I had
followed that path, we would never have had any A.A. Somebody had to be out in front and have a first name and a last name
and a mailing address and a post office box and a listed
telephone. Neither Dr. Bob nor I saw the necessity for such
anonymity. They'd never had any in the Oxford Group. [For
more on the views of Dr. Bob and other early AAs on
anonymity, see *DR. BOB and the Good Oldtimers*, pp. 164-65.]

Like Dr. Bob, Clarence did not view the Twelve Traditions
with favor—particularly the Eleventh Tradition pertaining to
anonymity. Clarence always pointed out that he simply shared his
own experience, strength, and hope in the A.A. Fellowship, and
that anonymity was not a part of that experience. He frequently
commented that anyone in A.A. could remain anonymous if they
wanted to and that many did want to remain anonymous in order
to keep their jobs secure. He pointed out that in the A.A. of the
1930's, jobs were scarce and that many employers would have
nothing to do with those who identified themselves as alcoholics
or members of Alcoholics Anonymous. Clarence pointed to
another reason for anonymity. Some of the early AAs were
lawyers, physicians, and bankers who were concerned that they
might be pestered by the many hundreds who were pouring into
A.A. in those days and might demand an undue amount of time
from those whose names and addresses they could find. By
contrast, both Dr. Bob and Clarence used their full names with
much frequency because they wanted to be available to those who
needed help.

On Tuesday, June 26, 1979, Clarence—the man who "went
from a banker to a skid row bum"—appeared before the American
Institute for Public Service, chaired by Jacqueline Kennedy Onassis
and Senator Robert Taft, Jr. The ceremonies took place at the East
Conference Room of the Supreme Court. Clarence, Grace, Steve
and his wife Sue and their children, were joined there by about
half a dozen other AAs and their families. Actor Kirk Douglas
presented Clarence with the Jefferson Award—a gold medallion

which stated it was given "in recognition of outstanding public service." It bore the embossed inscription of Mrs. Onassis, Senator Taft, and the Institute's president, Samuel S. Beard.

The statement of purpose (which accompanied the award) stated it was "to honor the highest ideals and achievements in the field of public service in the United States." Clarence's category honored him for "the greatest public service performed by private individuals benefitting local communities."

Part 2

As Grace Recalls

[The author and his son Ken spent a week in December of 1995 with Grace at her home in Florida, interviewing her and taping her remarks as well as reviewing her books and papers. Grace, the author, and Ken had all listened to a tape and observed a video of Clarence done in the 1980's. This portion of our book covers Grace's own recollections of what Clarence said—her memory often having been refreshed in part by the tape, video, and papers. Grace had specifically set out at the time of her marriage to Clarence to learn early A.A. history. She was present when Clarence related his knowledge of early A.A. to the representative of A.A. World Services who was writing an "official" account for AAs. Grace's recollections have been reviewed for accuracy and augmentation by three of Clarence's sponsees in Florida and by two in Wisconsin; and their recollections have, with Grace's approval, been added to flesh out the accounts Grace has provided.]

4

Clarence and A.A.'s
Founding Years

Sometime in the late 1970's, as Grace remembers it, Clarence received a phone call from Nell Wing in New York. Nell had come to A.A. General Services in the 1940's as a secretary. She became Bill Wilson's secretary, a good friend of Bill's wife Lois, and later A.A.'s first archivist. Nell said to Clarence: "Dr. Bob is dead. Bill Wilson is dead. And it is about time that the truth about early A.A. was told. We in New York do not know who the early people were. You know who those people are. And would you allow Niles P. [a member of the staff in New York] to come so that you can give Niles the knowledge that you have?" Clarence agreed.

Niles came to the home of Clarence and Grace in Florida via Greyhound Bus. He stayed with them in their home for a week. Grace was present throughout the interviews of Clarence by Niles concerning A.A.'s founding days and people. Niles continued to gather material, traveling around the United States by Greyhound Bus, and then returned to Florida one more time to discuss with Clarence and Grace what he had found during his travels.

The end result of this fact-gathering effort was A.A.'s Conference-Approved history titled *DR. BOB and the Good Oldtimers*—a book heavy with material about Dr. Bob and his wife Anne, Henrietta Seiberling, T. Henry and Clarace Williams, and

A.A.'s other Akron and Cleveland pioneers. And it was heavy with the specific recollections of Clarence S.

Prior to A.A.'s own history-gathering episode emanating from A.A.'s New York headquarters, Dr. Daniel J. Anderson (the President-Director of the Hazelden Foundation in Center City, Minnesota) had suggested to Clarence that Clarence write a book about early A.A.. Anderson said Hazelden would publish it. And Clarence had begun writing the history.

However, when *DR. BOB and the Good Oldtimers* was published, Clarence reached the conclusion and shared with others that "there was no necessity for my writing a history book because the truth had already been told in *DR. BOB and the Good Oldtimers*, and no further verification was needed." Clarence evidently held this view for the remainder of his life, for he often distributed copies of A.A.'s *DR. BOB* book, free of charge, to those attending the spiritual retreats he established and conducted in later years.

Our task here will therefore be to tell, as Grace recalls it, more fully about Clarence's relationship in the earliest years with Dr. Bob; with Anne Smith; and with the astonishing growth of early A.A. in Cleveland when Clarence founded, as he put it, "the first meeting of Alcoholics Anonymous" on May 11, 1939, at 2345 Stillman Road in Cleveland Heights, Ohio.

From one viewpoint, Clarence went through three phases of his relationship with Dr. Bob, Bob's wife Anne, and the total of some forty pioneers who had helped found A.A. by the time the writing of its Big Book had begun in 1938.

The first phase concerned what Clarence considered to be the providential way in which he met Dr. Bob. Clarence's sister-in-law Virginia had been seeing a Doctor Leonard Strong for medical help in New York. Clarence had been on the skids in New York, and Virginia asked Dr. Strong what could be done to help Clarence overcome his alcoholism. As it turned out, Doctor Strong was the brother-in-law of A.A.'s co-founder Bill Wilson. Doctor Strong had told Virginia (Clarence's sister-in-law) that there was a physician in Akron, Ohio, "who fixes drunks" and had achieved great success using the same spiritual techniques that had enabled Strong's brother-in-law Bill Wilson to recover from alcoholism. Virginia sent Clarence's wife, Dorothy, Dr. Bob's telephone number and address so that it would be available should Clarence return to Ohio and want to get sober.

Clarence did return to Cleveland, and his wife Dorothy gave him a one-way ticket to Akron and told him how to get in touch with Dr. Bob. Clarence saw Dr. Bob in his office but rejected Dr. Bob's plan to hospitalize him. Clarence was suffering from hallucinations and had some wild ideas about Dr. Bob's motives. He returned to Cleveland to live in hobo camps and under bridges and sink still further toward his bottom. But he did call Dr. Bob quite a number of times—clinging to the idea that this doctor could somehow, someday, help him to quit drinking.

Finally, Clarence met another bum whom he called a "flannel-mouthed Irishman." Clarence told that man that he wanted to quit drinking. The Irishman told Clarence that he (Clarence) was no damn good and would "die drunk." He told Clarence that he was too weak and had a chin just like Andy Gump. Clarence declared, "I'll show you. I know a doctor who can fix me." And he said the Irishman's challenging remarks fanned whatever little spark was left in him. Clarence returned to Akron to seek help from Dr. Bob.

Dr. Strong, Dr. Bob, and the Irishman had all helped sow the seed that brought Clarence to his all-important moment of clarity.

The second phase of Clarence's relationship with Dr. Bob began as he walked from the bus depot in Akron in snow three feet deep to Akron City Hospital—the place to which Dr. Bob had directed him. Upon arrival, Clarence fainted. He woke up in a hospital room in which the only literature was a Bible. Clarence managed to make it through the night without a drink; and the next day (February 11, 1938) marked the beginning of Clarence's first day of sobriety—a sobriety he maintained for forty-six years until the date of his death. He remained in Akron City Hospital for a total of six days.

Soon, two men visited Clarence in his hospital room. They introduced themselves, and said to him, "We have an answer to your problem." They told him the stories of their lives. They told him what had happened to them. And they showed him they were now sober. They said Clarence could have what they had if he wanted it. Whereupon, because Clarence was too weak to eat any food, they ate his lunch and departed.

Dr. Bob visited Clarence that afternoon (and every afternoon of Clarence's hospitalization). Two more drunks then appeared and told Clarence they too had an answer to his problem. They shared their stories. They ate his dinner. And they departed.

On the last day of Clarence's hospitalization, Dr. Bob sat on Clarence's bed; and the full story of what happened has yet to be told.

Dr. Bob finally gave Clarence the *answer* in this manner. The colloquy between Dr. Bob and Clarence is fully and correctly reported on page 144 of *DR. BOB and the Good Oldtimers*. The gist is as follows: Dr. Bob asked Clarence, "Do you believe in God, young fella?" Clarence equivocated. But Dr. Bob was insistent that Clarence give him a definitive answer. Clarence finally said that he did believe in God. Dr. Bob told him to get out of bed and on his knees, saying, "We're going to pray." Clarence said he didn't know how to pray, but Dr. Bob directed: "Just follow what I say, and that will do *for now*" (italics added). Clarence said he did what he was ordered to do.

What has been missing from this account is the fact that Clarence was then taken to his first Oxford Group meeting at T. Henry's house, *given a Bible by Dr. Bob*, and told by Dr. Bob to "go out and fix drunks as an avocation." This Clarence faithfully endeavored to do without any success whatever. Clarence returned to Cleveland to the streets where he had been a bum. He would wave his Bible in the faces of the derelicts and ask them if they wanted to be like him. *That* message did not "take."

Grace believes Clarence continued his witnessing efforts for at least seven months—all the while himself attending Oxford Group meetings in Akron and receiving vigorous Bible instruction from

Dr. Bob's wife Anne Smith. And it is not amiss here to point out that A.A.'s co-founder Bill Wilson and Clarence both described Anne Smith as the "Mother of A.A."

The final phase of Clarence's relationship with Dr. Bob in those earliest days was a happy and fruitful one.

One day, Clarence came to an Oxford Group meeting at the T. Henry Williams home in Akron. Clarence was in a state of despair over his inability to convert drunks. Dr. Bob said to him, "Young fella, it's about time you made your surrender." Clarence was bewildered. He said, "What is *that*, Doc?" Dr. Bob said, "You'll see when this meeting is over." What followed at the end of the meeting has not to our knowledge been recorded in A.A. literature thus far. For Clarence was about to become born again.

It has been told that Dr. Bob took Clarence upstairs to T. Henry's master bedroom. Grace recalls Clarence's saying that he went upstairs with Dr. Bob, T. Henry, and an Oxford Group member who was not an alcoholic. These men told Clarence to get on his knees, and they joined him on their knees around T. Henry's bed.

These three men then led Clarence through a "Sinner's Prayer." As Grace recalls it, Clarence described that prayer as follows:

Father, I come to you in Jesus's name. Lord Jesus, I am sorry for my sins. Please forgive me for every wrong thing I've ever done. I thank you for dying on the cross in my place. I ask you to come into my heart. Be the Lord of my life. And I will love you and serve you till you take me home.

Grace said the foregoing prayer was, in substance, the prayer Clarence used for the rest of his life as he took his sponsees through the subsequently-developed Third Step of Alcoholics Anonymous in which his sponsees "surrendered" and gave their lives to Jesus as Lord and Savior. Clarence often informed his sponsees that this surrender prayer was the very one Dr. Bob had used from the beginning of the A.A. surrenders in Akron.

The results for Clarence were electric. He surged forth once again with his Bible. This time, he had a message to carry. In very little time, Clarence was sponsoring fourteen men, which, after the custom of those days, he called "babies." Seven of these fourteen were Roman Catholics. Most or all had begun returning to their families and putting their lives together. The Roman Catholics were also confessing to a Roman Catholic priest in Cleveland. And Clarence was bringing them to the Wednesday night meetings of the Oxford Group at the T. Henry Williams home in Akron. The Cleveland contingent were part of what was then called the "alcoholic squad of the Oxford Group." In those days, the Oxford Group was also known as "A First Century Christian Fellowship," and Dr. Bob commonly referred to all of the meetings of the Akron group as a "Christian fellowship."

But the scene did not set well with the Roman Catholic priest in Cleveland. The story of the Cleveland contingent's break with the Akron group has been adequately reported in *DR. BOB and the Good Oldtimers* (see pages 156ff.) and elsewhere. In substance, the story relates that Clarence was informing Dr. Bob that the Cleveland contingent were finding themselves in an impossible situation. They were coming to Oxford Group meetings in Akron to save their lives from alcoholism; and the Roman Catholic priest was threatening them with excommunication if they continued to do so. Dr. Bob was standing firm that the alcoholics must choose to attend the Akron meetings if they wished to maintain sobriety. And Clarence was maintaining that something had to be done to make the program available to Roman Catholics without jeopardizing them with excommunication.

On May 10, 1939, Clarence announced at the Akron A.A. meeting that there would be a meeting the next night in Cleveland at the home of Al and Grace G. and that it would be for alcoholics only and their families. He said the name of the meeting would be taken from the Fellowship's just-published basic textbook "Alcoholics Anonymous."

The meeting *was* held—over the strenuous objections of Dr. Bob and an Akron contingent who attended the Cleveland meeting and remonstrated. From the day of that meeting on May 11, 1939, Clarence always maintained that he had founded the first genuine meeting of "Alcoholics Anonymous." Hence the origin of his controversial claim that he was the "founder" of Alcoholics Anonymous.

But, from the standpoint of the Fellowship of A.A., much good came of this Cleveland break-off. In the first place, Roman Catholics often claim there could have been no Catholics in A.A. but for Clarence's actions. In the second place, despite objections over Clarence's vigorous publicizing of the alcoholic meetings, the A.A. Fellowship grew from one to thirty groups in Cleveland within a year.

To the objection that Clarence had publicized A.A. by using his full name and that A.A. was intended to be an *anonymous* program of "attraction, rather than promotion," Clarence usually commented: "*Attraction?* Who would be *attracted* to drunks!"

A third salutary result came from the rapidly-growing Cleveland meetings. Dr. Bob did attend many; and when a survey of the membership in Cleveland was taken, it was found that some ninety-five percent of those alcoholics who "really tried," were achieving and maintaining sobriety. Clarence firmly believed the alcoholics had all they needed to proceed with their recovery program. Clarence said to Grace: They had the Big Book. They had the "Four Absolutes" of the Oxford Group. And they had the Holy Bible. And *all* were very much utilized in early Cleveland A.A.

Now for a few words Clarence shared with Grace about Dr. Bob's wife, Anne Ripley Smith, and about Dr. Bob himself.

Clarence said to Grace, "Anne was a mother to me." He said there were many things he would take to Anne that he did not feel free to take to Dr. Bob. For example, Grace said she knew that after Clarence got into the Oxford Group, there were many times in which he talked to Anne about how to handle his marriage relationship with Dorothy. Grace said she knew from Clarence's remarks that Dorothy had been the manager of the house and that things had changed when Clarence became the new focus. When the telephone calls began pouring in for Clarence, Dorothy felt left out.

Whatever Anne shared with Clarence in confidence was either never told to Grace or has slipped from her memory. However, one can appreciate the significance of Anne's advice to Clarence when he or she realizes that Bill Wilson asked Anne to write the section of the Big Book that came to be titled "To Wives." For Anne worked with alcoholics, their wives, and their whole families to help all of them recover from what later became recognized as a "family" disease.

Grace noted that Dr. Bob was a Vermonter. He was brusk, short, and to the point. He did not elaborate. As Clarence put it to Grace, "Doc just told you."

Dr. Bob was strict and stern. Clarence told the story about his going to Dr. Bob with the question, "What does 'First Things First' mean?" Dr. Bob answered, "It's in the Good Book. Look it up." Clarence read the whole Bible, and he could not find the answer. Back to Doc he went. Clarence said, "Doc, that phrase is not in the Bible." Doc said, "I'll tell you *this* time. It's 'Seek ye first the kingdom of God and his righteousness; and all these things shall be added unto you'" (See Matthew 6:33 and *DR. BOB and the Good Oldtimers*, p. 144). Doc then said, "From here on out, read that Bible and study it; and you'll know what's in it."

Grace said, "I don't remember any specific thing Clarence said Anne had taught him from the Bible. I do know she was a much softer, gentler person. She had patience and love. She really loved those men. And she took time to explain and talk to them, and teach them from the Word of God. Clarence made that clear to me."

Grace said, "Clarence was bowled over with Anne's compassion and love for a bunch of drunk men. [Furthermore,] she lived with one and put up with one." Dr. Bob himself often made similar remarks about Anne's patience and courage, and how she had put up with his condition for so many years. Grace added, "It would take a godly woman to do that. I'll bet she walked with one hand in God's." (For some first-hand recollections of Anne's love and service, see Dick B., *Anne Smith's Journal 1933-1939: A.A.'s Principles of Success*, pp. 3-17.)

In answer to the author's question whether Clarence said anything about the books Dr. Bob read, Grace said, "Yes. Dr. Bob often loaned Clarence books that he [Dr. Bob] read. And he was a stickler about loaning books. When Dr. Bob loaned a book, he wrote that down; and you couldn't get a second book, until you returned the first. Dr. Bob often questioned Clarence about what he had read. Doc wanted to be sure that it wasn't a drunk conning him into loaning books but not reading them. Dr. Bob wanted to be sure that Clarence was actually reading them."

Grace said she knew Clarence had a deep and abiding respect and love for Dr. Bob. What Dr. Bob said was gospel for Clarence.

Grace remembers Clarence's mentioning that he had read and studied the following books recommended by Dr. Bob:

Begbie's *Twice-Born Men*;
Brother Lawrence's *Practicing the Presence of God*;
Chambers' *My Utmost for His Highest*;
Clark's *I Will Lift Up Mine Eyes* and *Fishers of Men*;
Fosdick's three books—*The Meaning of Prayer*, *The Meaning of Faith*, and *The Meaning of Service*;
James' *The Varieties of Religious Experience*;
Kagawa's *Love: The Law of Life*;
Kempis's *The Imitation of Christ*;
Kitchen's *I Was a Pagan*;
Russell's *For Sinners Only*;
Shoemaker's *Children of the Second Birth* and *Twice-Born Ministers*;
St. Augustine's *Confessions*;
The Upper Room;
Walter's *Soul Surgery*; and
Weatherhead's *Discipleship*.

5

A.A.'s Roots in the Bible

Clarence left no doubt in anybody's mind that A.A. was grounded in the Bible. And four brief accounts illustrate that point.

First, we have already mentioned that when Clarence was hospitalized and achieved sobriety in February of 1938, the only piece of literature allowed and present in his hospital room was the Holy Bible. Also, as soon as Clarence had left the hospital and gone that evening to T. Henry's for his first Oxford Group meeting, Dr. Bob had then sent him on his way to Cleveland with a Bible that would help him "fix drunks."

The next incident impacted on Clarence and all who met him, including his wife Grace. At Clarence's early Oxford Group meetings at T. Henry's house, an A.A. pioneer named Bill V. H. had seemed to take a shine to Clarence. Bill had often backed Clarence into a corner behind T. Henry's library table. Bill had been in a mental hospital; and Clarence felt that perhaps the Oxford Group members were a bit leery of Bill. Clarence himself was also somewhat intimidated.

One night, while Bill had Clarence boxed in, Bill said, "Clarence, I have something to give you. And I want you to memorize it, read it, and never forget it." Clarence said Bill took out of his pocket this old, beat-up wallet with every kind of card in it and emptied it on the table. Clarence said that, as Bill scrambled around amongst the papers and cards, Bill found a little white folded piece of paper. He gave it to Clarence. On the piece of paper was just one Bible verse—2 Corinthians 5:17—which states: "Therefore if any man *be* in Christ, *he is* a new creature: old things are passed away; behold, all things are become new."

Clarence told Grace that he had kept that piece of paper for years and years and years until he wore it out. Clarence said, "That scripture changed my life." Furthermore, Clarence frequently wrote the passage down for others. He had it printed on the back of cards he passed out in A.A. and elsewhere. And the author was handed a card by Grace S. when he first met her. That card contained her name and address on one side and the same verse—2 Corinthians 5:17—on the back side of it.

Also, just as Dr. Bob had done, Clarence many times told others that A.A.'s basic ideas had come from Matthew chapters 5-7 (Jesus's Sermon on the Mount), 1 Corinthians 13 (the so-called "love" chapter), and the Book of James. Grace said Clarence told his babies to read those three segments; and Grace (as one of Clarence's babies) did just that. She said the reading was not *recommended* reading; it was *required*.

Finally—and also as Dr. Bob, the Oxford Group people, and the Akron AAs did—Clarence regularly referred to the Oxford Group's "Four Absolutes." Those "Four Standards," as they were also called in the Oxford Group, were used as "yardsticks" for measuring how one conducted one's life daily from a moral standpoint.

The Four Absolutes had first been assembled by Oxford Group progenitor, Dr. Robert E. Speer, from the teachings of Jesus Christ. Some in the Oxford Group thought the Four Absolutes—honesty, unselfishness, purity, and love—had been taken by Dr. Speer from the Sermon on the Mount itself. The Biblical origins of the Four Absolutes in the *New Testament* are very clear, but Speer took the Standards from several of the Gospels. And they were also found confirmed by Speer's successors in many other verses in the Church Epistles.

Clarence himself was first introduced to the Bible in Sunday School. He was frequently exposed to it at the missions where he said he had many times "given his life to Jesus" to get what he needed. Clarence's exposure to the Bible as an alcoholic seeking recovery began in earnest at the Oxford Group meetings where Bible study was regular fare. It continued at Doc and Anne Smith's on Saturdays and Sundays. He said that Anne always taught out of the Bible and that her favorite segment was the Book of James.

As Clarence's married life with Grace moved through the years, they both engaged in an hour of Bible study regularly. Clarence and Grace both owned and used *Strong's Exhaustive Concordance of the Bible* to aid them in their studies.

There are at least four Bible verses which appear to have been basic in A.A. Three of them are quoted verbatim in the Big Book, and the fourth was very commonly quoted by Anne Smith to early AAs and their families. Interestingly, Grace said Clarence never mentioned to her that Dr. Bob had asked him to memorize particular verses in the Bible. Yet he was very clear that Anne Smith had done exactly that.

The four basic verses in A.A.'s background are the following:

God is love. (1 John 4:8,16)

Grace said that Clarence covered that idea about as well as she had ever heard it covered. Clarence said that he had grown up thinking of God in the abstract as a tall figure in the wild blue yonder with a notebook recording dirty things he had done. Clarence said, "He is my Father. He loves me. And He cares about everything about me." And Clarence called Him, "My loving Father."

Love thy neighbor as thyself. (James 2:8)

Grace said she and Clarence talked about this concept many times. She said, "We agreed we had to love a kid we sponsored, related to, or were going to be around in A.A. exactly like Jesus Christ loved us when we were lost in our sins and trespasses."

Thy will be done. (Matthew 6:10)

Grace said:

I learned early in my life, and from Clarence, and in my married
life, not to pray for foolish, silly things for myself. I do pray for
myself, and Clarence prayed for himself. I know God knows my
needs. But I need to express to Him my needs. He expects that
of me. I was taught that prayer was talking and listening. If I
don't talk to God and wait for His answer, I'm not communicat-
ing with Him. A lot of people in A.A. that I sponsor will pray
up a storm—very voluble and vocal. Then they are up and
running. Never thinking about waiting for an answer. You have
to teach them.

Faith without works is dead. (James 2:20)

Grace said, "Clarence and I were agreed that we could sit and
teach kids all day long how to have faith and build their faith; but
if we didn't demonstrate that faith by doing, by living what we
were teaching, then faith without works is absolutely dead."
Having heard Grace's recollections about the foregoing verses
which are well-known to many AAs, the author had hoped to hear
from Grace herself many *more* of the direct links between
particular A.A. Steps and particular Bible verses. Grace herself
was not readily able to recall such verses; but Steve F.—who was
Clarence's sponsee and worked alongside Grace at Clarence's
retreats—was able to provide the author with a number of verses
Clarence commonly quoted in connection with some of the
particular steps. And then Grace confirmed the historical reliability
of Steve's recollections.
And A.A.'s biblical roots from the early Akron days seem
clearly defined: (a) because of what Clarence told Grace about the
Bible's use in early A.A.; (b) because of the work that Grace
reported that she and Clarence did *together* in A.A.; and (c)
because of the work she herself does *today* in A.A. All these facts

vividly underline what was passed to Grace through Clarence from early A.A.

Grace said she and Clarence seldom took their kids through the Twelve Steps without copies of the Big Book and the Good Book at their sides. She said, "We used them both—always." She gave several examples of what they did with the kids in this respect.

If a sponsee came to Clarence and indicated that a problem had arisen over gossip, Clarence would open to the Book of James and quote, as Dr. Bob and Anne had both done, the language to which a major portion of James, chapter 3, is devoted. James 3:5-6 state:

> Even so the tongue is a little member and boasteth great things. Behold, how great a matter a little fire kindleth! And the tongue *is* a fire, a world of iniquity: so is the tongue among our members, that it defileth the whole body and setteth on fire the course of nature; and it is set on fire of hell.

In his very last address to AAs, Dr. Bob cautioned AAs to guard against "that erring member the tongue." And Clarence taught that lesson well to his babies.

Another example involved James 5:16 where, in speaking of the Fifth Step, Clarence often quoted the verse, "Confess *your* faults one to another and pray for one another, that ye may be healed."

The evidence that Matthew 5:23-24 in Jesus's Sermon on the Mount impacted on A.A. is somewhat less clear. Matthew 5:23-24 was commonly quoted in the Oxford Group as to the necessity for making restitution. The quote also appeared in A.A. literature and in the memorial article published by the *A.A. Grapevine* at the time of Dr. Bob's death. Grace said she was quite familiar with the verses and couldn't help but believe that they had been used in teaching kids about amends. The verses read: "Therefore if thou bring thy gift to the altar, and there rememberest that thy brother hath ought against thee; leave there thy gift before the altar, and go thy way; first be reconciled to thy brother, and then come and offer thy gift."

Clarence often referred to particular verses in the Sermon on the Mount that had given rise to certain well-known A.A. slogans. One slogan, "First Things First," has just been discussed. Dr. Bob said this slogan came from Matthew 6:33 ["But seek ye first the kingdom of God, and his righteousness"]. Clarence passed this biblical vignette along to his babies.

Another slogan, "Easy Does It," came, said Dr. Bob, from Matthew 6:25 and 6:34 [also part of the Sermon on the Mount]. The gist of these verses is that one should not be anxious for the morrow or for what he or she shall eat, drink, or wear; for God provides all these things—feeding even the birds of the air and clothing the lilies of the field. The same verses from Matthew chapter 6 also gave rise, said Dr. Bob, to the slogan, "One Day at a Time." The Sermon on the Mount said "the morrow shall take thought for the things of itself. Sufficient unto the day *is* the evil thereof." And Clarence passed along this historical item to the people he sponsored.

We will soon see other verses Clarence mentioned from the Bible as he took people through particular A.A. Steps.

Clarence's Bible Stories

Clarence's kids loved to hear him tell Bible stories; and the author has met several of Clarence's sponsees who independently verified that Clarence's stories were popular. The stories demonstrated Clarence's detailed knowledge of the Bible, his sense of humor, and his ability to draw an audience's attention to the Bible by telling a story about it. Here in brief are three of his well-known stories.

Noah

Clarence said the Bible is full of rummy stories. He often talked about Noah. The story goes like this:

Noah was a rummy. Noah—"the guy that had the boat." The world was hell-bent for disaster. God couldn't get people off their kick. He decided to flood the world and start all over. Noah trusted God and loved Him. God said, "Build a boat." He gave him the dimensions. He told him to put two of every creature in there—male and female. Wonder why those two mosquitos got in? Noah worked for a hundred years. He built a boat in the middle of the desert. People kept asking him why. It rained forty days and forty nights. People tried to get in. Noah couldn't open the door. The boat floated. The boat settled on Mt. Ararat. The first thing Noah did was to plant a vineyard, raise grapes, make some wine, and get drunk. Noah was a rummy. (See Genesis 6:9-9:21).

The Good Samaritan

A priest was coming down the road, and he saw a man lying in a ditch drunk. And he said, "Good enough for him." And he passed on the other side. Another man came down the road. And he was a Levite. And he saw the man lying in the ditch drunk. But he too passed on the other side. Then the third man, a Samaritan, came and saw the man in the ditch. And he got down from his conveyance—I don't think it was a Ford—and he poured oil and wine in his wounds and bound them up. Then he took him in his arms and put him on his form of conveyance and took him to the Holiday Inn. And he said to the innkeeper, "You take this man and take care of him. And here's some money. And if you need any more, when I come back by, I'll pay you anything he owes you." I knew the Samaritan was a traveling salesman because he told the innkeeper, "When I come back next time, if there be any more due, I'll pay you." Which one did the right thing for the rummy? (See Luke 10:25-37.)

The Prodigal Son

There was a Jewish man who had two sons. It was a custom among Jews at that time, that when a father got old, he would divide his estate among the boys. Now the older son was the Al-Anon. He did everything his dad told him to. But the younger

one—you know who—always badgered his dad for his share of
the loot. Finally, the younger kid just got tired, and he wanted
his right now. The father just couldn't take it any more and gave
it to him and said, "Take it and be gone." The Bible said that he
wandered into a far off country and spent his money in riotous
living. There came a famine in the land. And then he came to
himself and said, "I starve. And my father has much. And I
don't eat what the hogs eat. I eat the husks of the hogs." He had
become what no Jewish kid would become. He was a nursemaid
to a bunch of hogs. And he said, "I'll go to my father, and I'll
fall at his feet. And I'll tell him I'm unworthy. And I'll work as
a hired hand for him." Now I am going to tell you the only
record in the Bible where God ran. And the father saw him
coming a far off. And he ran to meet him. And he fell on his
neck. And he kissed him. And he said, "My son who was dead
is alive. Bring the ring to put on his finger." The ring was for
authority. "Shoes on his feet and the cloak on his back." And he
cried, "My son who was dead is alive. Kill the fatted calf. Let's
have a party." And the older brother was working out in the field
and heard all the ruckus up at the house. And he stopped one of
the servants and asked him what was going on up at the house.
And the servant said, "Oh, haven't you heard? Your brother has
come home." And the brother said, "Oh, that no good . . . He
took his money and squandered it on loose living. He never gave
a party for me." Wasn't that just human? And his father had to
talk to him and straighten him out and tell him that the brother
that was dead was alive, and they were celebrating.

The Prodigal Son story is a story of redemption. (See Luke
15:11-32.)

Clarence said there were lots of rummy stories in the Bible.

Psalm 91

"AA of Akron" published a pamphlet titled *A Manual for
Alcoholics Anonymous*. The Akron pamphlet stated that it

was written and edited by members of Alcoholics Anonymous of Akron, Ohio, . . . among [whose] Akron members are one of the founders, the first person to accept the program, and a large number of other members whose sobriety dates back to 1935, 1936, and 1937.

According to A.A. historian Wally P., this pamphlet was one of four Akron pamphlets published during the 1940's. Each was written by Evan W. at the request of Dr. Bob. Dr. Bob asked Evan to write some "Blue Collar" literature to simplify the program for the average AA coming into the fellowship at that time.

The pamphlet stated:

There is the Bible that you haven't opened for years. Get acquainted with it. Read it with an open mind. You will find things that will amaze you. You will be convinced that certain passages were written with you in mind. Read the Sermon on the Mount (Matthew V, VI, VII). Read St. Paul's inspired essay on love (I Corinthians XIII). Read the Book of James. Read the Twenty-Third and Ninety-First Psalms. These readings are brief but so important.

Until recently, the author had not known that the Twenty-Third and the Ninety-First Psalms had been credited with so much importance by the early Akron AAs.

But, as the reader will shortly see, Clarence and Grace very frequently referred to the Twenty-Third Psalm. Clarence read it and requested that it be read the day he died. Grace said she and Clarence also accorded the Ninety-First Psalm great significance. They even sang a portion of it in the Assembly of God church they attended. When the author asked Grace for her favorite segment of the Bible, she immediately replied, "the Ninety-First Psalm."

To give our reader a sense of the comfort and encouragement the Ninety-First Psalm provides, we quote it here:

He that dwelleth in the secret place of the most High shall abide under the shadow of the Almighty.

I will say of the Lord, *He is* my refuge and my fortress: my God; in him will I trust.

Surely he shall deliver thee from the snare of the fowler, *and* from the noisome pestilence.

He shall cover thee with his feathers, and under his wings shalt thou trust: his truth *shall be thy* shield and buckler.

Thou shalt not be afraid for the terror by night; *nor* for the arrow *that* flieth by day;

Nor for the pestilence *that* walketh in darkness; *nor* for the destruction *that* walketh at noonday.

A thousand shall fall at thy side, and ten thousand at thy right hand; *but* it shall not come nigh thee.

Only with thine eyes shalt thou behold and see the reward of the wicked.

Because thou hast made the Lord, *which is* my refuge, *even* the most High, thy habitation;

There shall no evil befall thee, neither shall any plague come nigh thy dwelling.

For he shall give his angels charge over thee, to keep thee in thy ways.

They shall bear thee up in *their* hands, lest thou dash thy foot against a stone.

Thou shalt tread upon the lion and adder: the young lion and the dragon shalt thou trample under feet.

Because he hath set his love upon me, therefore will I deliver him: I will set him on high, because he hath known my name.

He shall call upon me, and I will answer him: I *will be* with him in trouble; I will deliver him, and honour him.

With long life will I satisfy him, and shew him my salvation.

6

The Oxford Group Ideas and Influence

Clarence frequently said:

> We owe our origin to the Oxford Group. But they were all
> "civilians." I saw friction between the "earthlings" and the
> "rummies." Due to a number of reasons, we had to break out
> and start on our own. Mainly because of religion. No one here
> is against religion, I hope. But the Oxford Group was a
> Protestant religious fellowship . . . and the Catholic Church
> didn't allow them [AAs] to . . . [attend]. We grew out of the
> Oxford Movement [Clarence here meant the "Oxford *Group*."
> The Oxford Group was also frequently called "A First Century
> Christian Fellowship"]. We had a program presented to us that
> worked. We had the answer.

At this point, the author should explain, compare, and contrast
the two most frequently mentioned origins of A.A. ideas.

The first was the Bible. Clarence said very plainly,
"Everything in this program came from the Bible." Dr. Bob said,

> The early AAs were convinced that the answer to their problems
> was in the Good Book. . . . We already had the basic ideas.
> . . . We got them . . . as a result of our study of the Good Book.
> (*DR. BOB and the Good Oldtimers*, pp. 96-97).

43

Anne Smith, Dr. Bob's wife, said, "Of course, the Bible ought to be the main Source Book of all. No day ought to pass without reading it" (Dick B., *Anne Smith's Journal, 1933-1939*, p. 80). For a complete discussion of A.A.'s roots in the Bible, see Dick B., *Dr. Bob's Library: Books for Twelve Step Growth*; *Anne Smith's Journal, 1933-1939: A.A.'s Principles of Success*; and *The Good Book and The Big Book: A.A.'s Roots in the Bible*.

The second and much more frequently credited source of A.A. ideas was the Oxford Group. Bill Wilson's biographer said: "They (Bill and Bob) tried to base everything they did, every step they took toward formulating their program, on Oxford Group principles" (Thompson, *Bill W.*, p. 239). Bill himself finally said that early AAs had learned:

> about moral inventory, amends for harm done, turning our wills and lives over to God . . . meditation and prayer and all the rest of it . . . from Dr. Bob's and my own earlier association with the Oxford Groups [sic] as they were then led in America by that Episcopal rector, Dr. Samuel Shoemaker. (*The Language of the Heart*, p. 298).

Bill dubbed Sam Shoemaker a "co-founder" of A.A. (See Dick B., *Design for Living*, p. 16). In his Oxford Group pamphlet, Sam Shoemaker's friend, the Reverend Sherwood Day, stated, "The principles of 'the Oxford Group' are the principles of the Bible" (Day, *The Principles of the Group*, p. 1). For a complete study and discussion of the Oxford Group influence on early A.A., see Dick B., *Design for Living: The Oxford Group's Contribution to Early A.A.* and *New Light on Alcoholism: The A.A. Legacy from Sam Shoemaker*.

A.A.'s Bible and Oxford Group origins may seem to some to be separate, distinct, and even contradictory. But it is the author's view they can be understood and harmonized in the following manner.

First, let's look at *structure*. The Oxford Group had a structure involving groups, teams, a fellowship, story-telling, and the sharing of individual success experiences (as distinguished from the rendering of opinions). Similarly, the Bible-studying "alcoholic squad of the Oxford Group" in Akron had its *group* ("Akron Number One"), *teams* that visited drunks, the Oxford Group *fellowship* itself, and the *sharing of experiences.*

There was no similar "squad"—or at least not a group that was called a squad—among New York's early Oxford Group members. But the New Yorkers did attend Oxford groups, work together as teams, belong to the Oxford Group fellowship, and (perhaps in a less organized fashion) share their experience.

The Bible was definitely the center of the experience. Oxford Group founder, Dr. Frank N. D. Buchman, was, as his own people described him, "soaked in the Bible." He arranged Bible study for Oxford Group adherents. Sam Shoemaker in New York was, as his biographer described him, a "Bible Christian." And Shoemaker focused on the Bible and Bible study in his books, meetings, and teachings.

The author's own research—involving study of hundreds of books that early AAs read (when coupled with the statements by Dr. Bob, Anne Smith, and Clarence that the A.A. program came from the Bible)—justifies the conclusion that the Bible verses and principles which underlie the language in the Big Book and the Twelve Steps came directly from early A.A.'s study of the Bible, Bible devotionals, and Christian literature of the day. Moreover, Bible study, the use of Bible devotionals, and the reading of Christian literature (in large part literature of Oxford Group writers themselves) were all part and parcel of the Oxford Group life-changing program. Hence, we believe it fair to say that *both the Bible itself and the Oxford Group's structure and biblical principles did* underlie all of the major ideas the early A.A. fellowship borrowed from "religion" (more specifically, from the Bible; and even more specifically, from Christianity).

In this portion of our book on Grace and Clarence, we will focus on Clarence's frequent mention of, and familiarity with, the Oxford Group program and principles, as he explained them to Grace and many others.

We will see in the next chapter that Clarence frequently divided his discussion of the Twelve Steps into four parts. He said the Steps involved: (1) admission, (2) submission, (3) restitution, and (4) construction. Clarence then discussed the Steps in sequence as they fit under the four segments.

Similarly, after several years of research and submitting his conclusions for review by living Oxford Group people, the author was able to divide into eight segments twenty-eight Oxford Group principles which the author verified as having influenced A.A. And, within the framework of the eight Oxford Group segments, we will here review Clarence's often stated comments on the Oxford Group program as Clarence discussed it with Grace and others.

As stated, our review will be within the framework of the eight major Oxford Group categories we have previously fashioned and now set forth below for discussion purposes.

God

Clarence was very disturbed—as the author himself has been—with the absurd names for God that have appeared within the A.A. Fellowship in its recent years. Clarence often pointed to such names for A.A.'s "Higher Power" as the "Group," "a piano," and "a lightbulb." Clarence reduced his critical comments to writing in his pamphlet titled *My Higher Power—The Lightbulb*.

Grace thought this was the only pamphlet Clarence ever wrote. But we learned that Clarence also wrote a pamphlet titled *Going Through the Steps*—an historical matter we will discuss in a later chapter. We consider the contents of *My Higher Power—The Light Bulb* to be so significant that we quote it below in full:

My Higher Power—The Lightbulb by Clarence S.

In their sincere and honest attempt to maintain a "hands off policy" regarding fellow members' religious beliefs and perhaps sensitivities, our founding fathers exercised gentle wisdom and proffered spiritual freedom. No one, it was rightly thought, should be permitted to impose their own religious concepts and beliefs upon any other member of the fellowship. The area was much too important to the prospective recoveree to be tampered with by mortal man. The life of the prospect depends, ultimately, upon his or her "personal relationship" with a "Power greater than themselves." The notion was valid in the Program's earlier days—and it still is!

In no way, shape or form, however, was the idea conceived to avoid guiding our beloved newcomer along the path of spiritual progress. Quite the contrary, our whole purpose as recovered alcoholics, was and is to help the next person achieve sobriety. If that person is a *real* alcoholic his only hope is God. So in its most basic and simplest terms our only real purpose is to help the still-suffering alcoholic to find God. A loving God, a healing God is the alcoholic's only real hope.

This is no easy task. A vast array of difficulties present themselves to thwart the new person on his journey. The foremost adversary, of course, is the illness itself. It seems that many, many alcoholics have a very fierce, emotionally charged resistance to accepting any dependency upon a Power which, to them, may seem an abstract and remotely distant concept. This internal resistance is most effectively broken down by the potential recoveree's initial desperation. (It seems such a shame that today's A.A. actually encourages the newcomer to avoid reaping the blessings of that desperation.) If intense enough and deep enough, this emotional "bottom" will be the very propellant the prospect needs to thrust him into the recovery process offered by A.A. through its 12 steps.

Another stumbling block, which many people who are new to the Program are currently encountering, is us! We seem to be full of fear as regarding the responsibility we have been given in the area of spiritual guidance. We shirk this responsibility by evasiveness or by the direct side-stepping of the issue by such statements as, "It's 'God as *you* understand him' and it's up to you to come to your own conclusions." So the newcomer is left to his own devices. He is expected to arrive, alone and unguided, at a relationship with his Creator.

One of the most powerful and hope-filled statements to be found in the entire text of *Alcoholics Anonymous* can be found on page 25. "The great fact is just this, and nothing less: That we have had deep and effective spiritual experiences which have revolutionized our whole attitude toward life, toward our fellows and towards God's universe. The central fact of our lives today is the absolute certainty that our Creator has entered into our hearts and lives in a way which is indeed miraculous. He has commenced to accomplish those things for us which we could never do by ourselves." Are we, today, so far removed from our founders' results of our recovery program that these words are nothing more than a "nice thought" and an exaggeration due to artificially elated emotions? If so, we "obviously cannot transmit something we don't have." We cannot share awareness we don't have. Cannot give guidance we have never gotten. We cannot share a vision of a God we have never seen. Our lack, thereby, becomes the newcomer's, and he may die because of it!

Our resistance becomes his license. In his liquor befogged mind he does not seek and experience God but begins to "create." It's no wonder his dryness becomes so barren that in a short while he returns to drink. His "Higher Power" was a lightbulb! (No joke. We have heard this concept voiced more than once, and not only by a newcomer!) Or perhaps this power greater than himself was a chair, or a wall, or even a mortal sponsor. A quick glance at the top of page 93 of the "Big Book" makes instantly clear a very important qualification in the concept of ". . . as you understand Him," and that is: "he can choose any conception he likes, PROVIDED IT MAKES SENSE TO HIM."

Power greater than himself—a lightbulb? A simple flick of a switch turns off that power. A wall? Not so powerful when confronted with a bulldozer. A chair? An axe can make quick kindling of that higher power. A sponsor then? If he fails to perfect his spiritual life, his old foe alcohol is sure to reclaim him. So he won't do very well as a greater power. How about a whole group? Possibly for someone else, but not for us. If one person who is powerless over alcohol is joined by another who is powerless over alcohol, and another, and another, we would have a group of people who are powerless over alcohol. We do not have a group of people who are POWERFUL over alcohol. They do not drink because they have gained access to something more powerful than alcohol—the Power of God.

It was never intended that phrases such as "higher power," "power greater than ourselves," or "as we understood Him" were created as an enabling device to justify our membership's continued avoidance of a connection with our Creator. Page 46 of the AA book says, "We found that as soon as we were able to lay aside prejudice and express even a willingness to believe in a Power greater than ourselves, we commenced to get results, even though it was impossible for any of us to fully define or comprehend that Power which is God." Again, ". . . that Power which is God." Our founders held no reservations, whatsoever, with Who was dealing with them. Perhaps we would be well advised to think twice before we attempt any ourselves. Alcoholics Anonymous is not allied with any religion as we well know. But it is allied with God, "For our very lives as ex-problem drinkers depend on it." It is allied with spirituality for despite what our Preamble states, A.A. is not a "fellowship;" it is a spiritual way of life.

It is our most earnest desire that no one reading this feel that we are trying to impose any presentation of God of [sic] His nature on anyone. Our real hope is that a reader may be jolted from a position of complacency or spiritual evasion and get about the business of recovery.

In a tape (to which the author listened), Clarence elaborated on the absurdity of calling God a "lightbulb." Clarence read through each of the Twelve Steps, but substituted the word "lightbulb" for the word "God" and for words which referred to God.

For example, in dealing with Step Two, Clarence would read, "Came to believe that a Lightbulb could restore us to sanity." As to Step 3, "Made a decision to turn our will and our lives over to the care of a Lightbulb." As to Step Five, "Admitted to a Lightbulb, to ourselves, and to another human being the exact nature of our wrongs." As to Step Seven, "Humbly asked a Lightbulb to remove our shortcomings." And so on.

The Bible, said Clarence, declared that God is the "*Creator.*"
Clarence so defined God. So did the Oxford Group. And so did
the Big Book in several places. (See Big Book, pp. 13, 25, 28, 56,
68, 72, 75, 76, 80, 83, 158, 161.)

Concerning God, the Oxford Group commonly said, "God has
a plan." Grace often heard Clarence use this expression. The
Oxford Group also said, "Man's chief end was to do God's will."
Grace said Clarence declared that God's plan was "that we live for
Him, serve Him, and live according to His Word as He taught it."
The Oxford Group also said that their life-changing process had to
start with a belief that God *is*. And Grace said both Clarence and
Dr. Bob were emphatic about that same point. God is!

Sin

The Oxford Group considered sin to be a reality and defined it as
anything that blocks us from God and another person.

Grace said it was fair to say that Clarence, like the speaker
President Cal Coolidge heard, would have said about sin, "I'm
against it." Clarence often said that God does not hold sin against
you. Clarence added that "God isn't a celestial Santa Claus to
whom you can run away and say I'm sorry. You have to repent
and turn away from sin." The Oxford Group frequently said you
must "hate and forsake sin." Grace pointed out that Clarence tried
to live a sinless life as much as a human person could, and that he
tried as much as he could to live by the sinless principles of the
Oxford Group's Four Absolutes.

Surrender

The Oxford Group summarized its life-changing program in terms
of making a surrender, utilizing "soul surgery" to accomplish the
surrender, and then achieving a "life-change" as the result.

Grace said she had heard Clarence use all these terms. She told
the author that Clarence often said:

If I hadn't surrendered my life and my problems to God, I'd
have tied His hands behind His back. I needed to release my life
and my problems, and untie His hands so that He could operate
in my life.

The Life-Changing Program Itself

Decision

As in A.A., the Oxford Group life-change process started with a
"decision." Grace said Clarence spoke of two kinds of decisions.
The first required a newcomer to make a decision that he would go
to any lengths to get sober—a decision he made before beginning
the Steps. The second was the decision the A.A. newcomer made
on his knees—while taking the Third Step—and praying the
"Sinner's Prayer."

Self-Examination

Clarence often spoke of the importance of a "moral inventory."
The Oxford Group and Anne Smith both used the Oxford Group's
Four Absolutes as yardsticks for "making the moral test." Grace
vividly recalls Clarence's belief that one should measure his life in
light of the Four Absolutes.

Confession

The Oxford Group, as well as Clarence and other early AAs, all
appear to have agreed beyond question that life-changing required
the confession called for in James 5:16.

Conviction

Oxford Group people often spoke of the necessity for being "con-
victed of sin." Grace said Clarence believed A.A. went astray
when it started using every conceivable word *but* "sin." (See *Pass*

It On, p. 197, for an example of the use of the word "sins" in
A.A.'s original six Steps.) Clarence objected to such statements as,
"I have a 'disease.'" Clarence said, "I know what God calls
it—'sin!'" He felt A.A. should not have adopted such watered
down expressions as "wrongs," "defects of character," and
"shortcomings." Grace added Clarence's believed in the biblical
injunction about the "sin"—"And be not drunk with wine, wherein
is excess; but be filled with the Spirit" (Ephesians 5:18).

Conversion

Oxford Group writers often insisted, as did Jesus in John 3:7, "Ye
must be born again." Clarence very frequently added the
expression from John 14:6 that there is no access to God but
through His Son—"no man cometh unto the Father, but by me."

Restitution

The Oxford Group said the life-changing process meant little
unless one set right the wrongs he had caused. Clarence said
similarly, "You can't get well unless you clear up the wreckage of
the past."

Jesus Christ

The Oxford Group had many ways of discussing and many
expressions for the power received through the accomplishments
of Jesus Christ. Oxford Group founder Frank Buchman often put
it this way, "Sin, Jesus Christ and (the result) a miracle."

Grace recalled very well a talk Clarence had made in Portland,
Oregon. He had delivered a sketch of the Twelfth Step. He
concluded his talk saying: "Kids. There's only one answer to all
your problems on this earth and that's God's Son Jesus Christ."

Spiritual Growth

In one sense, the Oxford Group collected under the heading "Conservation" most of the ideas it suggested for spiritual growth; and it later changed this category to "Continuance." This idea of "Continuance" was the fifth of the Oxford Group's "Five C's" about which Dr. Bob, Anne, and other early AAs often spoke.

The first Oxford Group "C" was "Confidence." It involved not only the Twelfth Step idea of gaining the confidence of a newcomer by sharing drinking experiences, but also keeping in confidence and sharing experience with the newcomer about the sins or shortcomings confessed in the Fifth Step. The second "C" was "Confession," about which we have just spoken. The third and fourth "C's" were "Conviction" and "Conversion" about which we have also just spoken. Grace said she did not believe Clarence discussed the fifth "C"—"Continuance"—or actually used that word. She said Clarence often mentioned that when one had completed the first nine Steps, the final job was "Construction"—"building a new life." The next few categories reflect Clarence's statements, as supplemented by those of Grace, concerning various aspects of Oxford Group "Continuance" (or "Construction" as Clarence put it).

Daily Surrender

Clarence said, "This is how you establish and maintain your connection with God and your ability to be of service in A.A. and with the kids you sponsor." Grace said, "Clarence was a great believer that you needed to walk the walk and also let your *conversation* provide evidence that you are *living* what you are talking about." Grace said, "I've heard a lot of talk within the rooms of A.A., but I've found a lot of people are not living what they were talking about in A.A. when they get out into society and into the world."

Guidance

Clarence said, "You must get your guidance in a quiet time with God." Grace said, "Clarence proved to me that it was essential to make room for quiet time and schedule your day so that you had a quiet time." She said Clarence's authority for that was the verse "Draw nigh to God, and he will draw nigh to you. . . ." (See James 4:8 and compare Big Book, p. 57: "When we drew near to Him He disclosed Himself to us!")

The Four Absolutes

Grace said of Clarence, "Clarence told me that in all of his life since he came into the Oxford Group, he planned his day to meet the requirements of absolute honesty, absolute purity, absolute unselfishness, and absolute love."

Absolute Honesty. As to absolute honesty, Grace said of Clarence: "There was no shaving or cutting absolute honesty." She said Clarence often told her, "Don't lend money to the kids; give it to them in your heart. Then there will be no grudges." Grace said, however, that many AAs are broke, that Clarence had a paycheck when he got his life straightened out, and that he frequently loaned the kids money.

She said she was astonished to see what happened when he opened his mail. She said: "There would be change falling out onto the table from toilet tissue into which it had been packed. He had taught his kids that they could not compromise on restitution; that they must go to the person they owed and offer to do work, or to be of service, or to repay what they owed." She said the money in the mail was an example of the rigorous honesty the kids were practicing in returning to Clarence the money he had loaned them. Clarence often told Grace and the kids, "If you are not scrupulously honest, you are only dry. You are not well. If you do not do a thorough housecleaning, it will come back to haunt you."

Absolute Purity. Clarence had much to say about absolute purity. Grace exclaimed, "Oh, that's a big one. And it's bigger today than it ever was." She said Clarence taught that absolute purity was to be measured according to God's standards, not man's. "It meant purity of the *mind* (no trashy junk or thinking) in their living actions."

Clarence often said, "The Absolute Standards followed the Ten Commandments." He would use the Ten Commandments as references, Grace said. Sometimes, kids would say the Ten Commandments aren't valid today. They would ask Clarence, "How can you be sexually pure?" And he would tell them, "You can't be without God's help. Impossible. So God must be your confidant. He knows your heart and your mind. It's just as important that we keep our mind clean; and since our body is the temple, we are not *told* to keep it clean. We are *commanded*."

Clarence often said that if you fall into immorality, all you have to do is go to God, confess your sins, and turn away from your sins. He said that none of us is perfect. Christ was the only perfect man. We will fall short. But the remedy for that is going back to God and asking for forgiveness and continually seeking that elusive perfectness that God used as a standard for us.

Clarence said Jesus Christ was our standard. And we are to model our life by His example. He said, "When you make a mistake, that is why they put erasers on lead pencils. You immediately go to God and ask Him for forgiveness, and He'll forgive you." When a kid asked, "How do I know that He'll forgive me?" Clarence would respond, "Because His Word says He will." (See 1 John 1:9.)

Absolute Unselfishness. As to absolute unselfishness, Grace said Clarence would look at who he was going to be with during that day, if he knew. He would look at where his appointments were and try to make sure he had no axe to grind. That there were no selfish motives that would benefit him in all of his dealings with that person. He would say, "Give the other fellow the benefit of doing business with a person who has nothing to gain—that is not looking for gain out of what he does. Our motives are to be by the heart."

Absolute Love. As to absolute love, Grace said, "Clarence and I tried to love the kids, our neighbors, and our friends exactly like Jesus Christ loved us. Jesus didn't tell me to get my act straightened up and then come to Him. He took me just like I was." Clarence often said, "If anybody doesn't understand the unquestioning love of God, they've missed a great deal. They've missed it if they can't love other people just like Christ loved us. Regardless of who they are, their station, or what they did to you. The criterion is 'love them like Jesus loved you.'"

Grace added, "That's why I take time with kids. I embrace them and hold them. Kids often come 400 miles to a retreat. They say, 'You know why I come? . . . Because you hold me in your arms. You take me just like I am. And I know that you love me.' I had a kid that always came alone to our retreat in Leesburg from Key West, Florida. She said, 'Grace, you know the reason I come? I come for the hugs and the love I get from you.' Love will break down all barriers. I know that love opens the door to their heart so that I can present the Lord to them."

Quiet Time

Grace said, "You do it in the morning. You know, God always walked with Adam in the morning. I'm sure their conversation was not always verbal. It was just conversation with each other heart to heart. Quiet time is where we improve our conscious contact with God. The Bible says, 'Be still, and know that I am God.' [See Psalm 46:10, which Clarence often quoted.] It's hard in the hectic life we live today. But it is essential to get your day started out right. You take the Bible and a writing pad. Often things will come that you know are from the Lord."

Bible Study

Grace said, "In the morning, Clarence and I alternated days in our Bible reading. At the breakfast table, we would read aloud to each other out of the Word. But then, in my day and in

Clarence's—when he had time—there was always Bible study individually. And listening to good teachings on television. I used to think television was the most evil thing because of the garbage on it. Then I learned I had an option. I could listen to the garbage or turn to a channel where they could teach me the Word. Now I often listen to six or eight Bible teachings during a day. Teachings from men of God I know are teaching it correctly. Some teach the Word; but they don't teach it correctly. So you have to be selective. T.V. can be evil, or it can be a great instrument enabling us to learn the Word of God."

Prayer

Grace said, "Essential. In the evening was my and Clarence's prayer time together. On our knees. And then, I always made time through the day as things arose from the kids. I needed to pray for direction. Sometimes not even on my knees. I depend on God for direction. I don't always follow, but I strive to do so.

"Today, I misplace things. But I learned something at my mother's knee. Her godmother was blind. Her godmother kept house and reared children; and she taught my mother that any time you misplace something and don't know where it is or can't find it, you ask the Holy Spirit to reveal where it is. I have a ninety percent success rate in finding what I've misplaced. It's just a feeling I have to check a certain place. God can and will if He is sought."

Listening and Writing Down Leading Thoughts

Grace said she and Clarence believed that if you don't do this when you listen and then take the time to write things down, you are apt to get busy and forget them.

Checking

Grace said she and Clarence believed emphatically that you have to know whether you have heard from God because Satan speaks to you through your ear gate and your eye gate. Grace said, "You have to check to know what your source of information is—whether it's the enemy or God. We have no defense against Satan. My mother used to say, 'An idle mind is the Devil's workshop.' It took me some time to know the truth of that statement because every deed we do originates in the mind. And sometimes you follow your Adversary if you don't check it out. The longer we practice this, the better we get. I need the feeling in my heart and the guidance of the Word of God."

The Spiritual Experience or Awakening

Knowledge of God's Will

Grace said, "Clarence taught that it is God's will for us to be happy, healthy, and prosperous. [See 3 John 2; and cp. Big Book, p. 133.] God's Word says that Satan comes to steal, to kill, and to destroy [See John 10:10]. I need to be ever aware of what my enemy does—how he approaches. I have no defense against Satan's programming things into my mind. My ears are open day and night. Clarence taught me to check thoroughly to see the source of my information. 'Be still, and know that I am God,' he said. You can talk and pray, but you must take time to get an answer. As to the will of God, I know the Bible is the inerrant, unchangeable will of God. That settles it."

God Consciousness

Grace said, "For me, it takes time—a walk with Him. I believe it comes automatically—that anything I do or say must be checked out with the Word of God. I ask Him to show me His perfect will in a person's life, and He'll direct me. But you have to ask. A lot of people know things intellectually, but they don't put them into practice. But that's what moves my life. I avoid hazards and pitfalls by relying on God's direction. So did Clarence."

Fellowship with God and Believers and Witness by Life and Word

Fellowship

Grace said, "About twenty years ago, I realized I didn't understand the Holy Spirit, and what I had available to me if I used it. I understood Jesus Christ intercedes for me with the Father. And since Jesus came into my heart, and I received the baptism of the Holy Spirit to empower me, I finally realized the power of the Holy Spirit. God and His Son, Jesus Christ, are as close to me as my hands and feet."

Witness by Life and Word

Clarence told Grace, "You will run dry and become stale if you don't 'give it away to keep it.'" Grace said, "I don't care who I have contact with, the first thing that comes into my heart is how I can witness to them. How can I witness Jesus Christ?

"For instance, I was standing in a line in a prescription drug store. There was quite a line. I saw a man who was in pain, and I spoke to him. I asked what he believed about healing the sick. I found out he was an Hungarian—ambivalent, but open. I asked him if I might pray with him. He said, 'At the *drug store*?' I said, 'Yes.' I took him behind the counter. I asked, 'Do you believe Jesus Christ can heal you just like when he walked on earth?' I felt he needed a little teaching, and I gave him an example from the Bible where Jesus said, '. . . Greater *works* than these shall he [the believer] do; because I go unto my Father' [See John 14:12]. I told him it was necessary for him to believe before I could heal him. I then asked him if I might anoint him with oil and pray for him.

He said, 'Oh, yes.' I did so. I never saw him again, but I know God heard my prayers."

7

The Big Book, Steps, and A.A. Fellowship

The Big Book

Clarence believed, as the author himself has heard so many in A.A. say, that A.A.'s basic text—the Big Book (the first 164 pages of *Alcoholics Anonymous*)—was divinely inspired. Grace added that she and Clarence had seen a number of efforts to rewrite the Big Book, one by two of Clarence's own sponsees. She observed that, in the case of Clarence's sponsees, the efforts were abandoned as the two men came to realize that their writing was "coming from their head and not from God."

When confronted with remarks criticizing A.A.'s co-founder Bill Wilson, Clarence sometimes turned the remarks aside. He said many times to Grace, "God used the very best that there was in those first less-than-forty men who contributed to the writing of the Big Book."

Concerning the Big Book, Clarence told Grace about a weekend trip Bill Wilson made to Akron, Ohio, to visit Dr. Bob shortly before Dr. Bob died. Year after year, Bill had been insisting to Dr. Bob that Bob endorse and "sign" A.A.'s Twelve Traditions. Bob had been declining, telling Clarence he (Bob) felt the Traditions had been written to hold power in New York.

Clarence said Dr. Bob called him down from Cleveland to be
present at the meeting with Bill because he (Clarence) supported
Dr. Bob's views.

On the occasion of the visit, Bill had the Twelve Traditions
with him. Bill said in Clarence's presence, "Doc, you've got to
sign these so I can add them to the Big Book." Dr. Bob replied,
"Bill, we have no need for what you call 'The Twelve Traditions.'
Our program came from the New Testament. We have the Bible.
We have the Four Absolutes. We have the Steps from the Oxford
Group. We've got the program. We just need to teach it as it is."

Clarence said Bill was insistent. Bill said, "Doc, you've got to
do it." Clarence said Bob was really exasperated. Bob finally said,
"All right. Give them to me. I've got to have some peace."
Clarence said Dr. Bob signed the paper and that shortly thereafter
the Twelve Traditions were "voted in" by A.A. Grace said
Clarence refrained from making a public issue of the matter. She
said, however, that whenever the Traditions were handed to
Clarence to read at a meeting, he would simply pass them on to
someone else.

Clarence told Grace there were only a few things in the Big
Book's basic text with which he disagreed. One concerned the
phrase, "God as we understood Him." As to the unacceptable
phrase "God as we understood Him," Clarence had this to say to
Grace: "The God that we understood when we wrote the Twelve
Steps was our Creator. And He was referred to over 200 times as
'God,' our Father—together with pronouns referring to Him in that
way." Clarence told Grace that it was this adamant position
concerning "God" that had caused the New Yorkers to call him
and Dr. Bob the "Bible thumpers."

The Big Book chapter 5—"How It Works"—commences with
this sentence, "Rarely have we seen a person fail who has
thoroughly followed our path." Clarence often said from the
podium, and to Grace, and to the people he sponsored that Bill
Wilson should not have used the word "rarely." He should have
said "Never," Clarence declared. Clarence said, "People who
thoroughly follow the path and do what it tells them to do *always*

succeed." Clarence took similar issue with the language on the next page of chapter 5. It states: "Here are the steps we took, which are suggested as a program of recovery. . . ." Clarence said, "There is no *suggestion* to it." Clarence never did "suggest" the Steps. He *told* the kids to take the Steps. Immediately! The Steps were *required*. Grace said Clarence maintained that position until he died. He never changed it.

The Twelve Steps

Grace often heard Clarence say that the Twelve Steps could be divided up into four categories: (1) admission, (2) submission, (3) restitution, and (4) construction. Clarence believed, said Grace, that Step One required "admission." Steps Two through Seven required "submission." Steps Eight and Nine required "restitution." And Steps Ten through Twelve required "construction." The last three Steps, said Clarence, required the AA to construct a new life. The AA was to judge his day in light of the last three Steps. Clarence believed that prayer, meditation, and study of the Word of God were the only way an AA could grow spiritually.

Speaking of the point in time at which she met Clarence, Grace said, "I was at a standstill." She said she had been taught as a child to memorize verses and sections of the Bible—often out of context. Her parents had taught her Psalm 119:11: "Thy word have I hid in mine heart, that I might not sin against thee." Her parents had stressed "memorize!" And Grace said she had followed directions and often could quote as many as fifty Psalms. She said things changed when she took the Steps with Clarence. She said, "I became a student at Clarence's knees. Clarence taught. We deepened our knowledge through our membership in the Assemblies of God churches. I [Grace] started *knowing* what the Word of God said."

Grace related what Clarence said to her and often repeated in his talks to AAs. *Clarence took people through the Twelve Steps in two days.* He gave the newcomer a week to ten days to get the alcohol out of his system. Then it was "go" as far as the Steps were concerned. Grace said when people would fly in to the home of Grace and Clarence, they were invited to stay for three days. Grace said that the "kids" needed to see how we did the Steps and practiced them in our life.

Grace gave an illustration of the pair's whole approach to the Steps. She said that in the 1970's she and Clarence had been on an A.A. speaking tour for ten days in New York. At one meeting, eighteen-to-twenty "tough kids" sat in the front "pew." They absorbed every word. In fact, the kids followed Clarence and Grace from meeting to meeting—everywhere they taught. She said twenty-seven of these "kids" had come in a motorcoach, a beat-up car, and motorcycles. Just before leaving New York, Grace announced that there was going to be a spiritual retreat at Brandon, Florida. It was called "Camp Florida."

The kids showed up at the Florida retreat without reservations. Grace said they had to put them up in the Admissions Office. She said their "guru" watched from the sidelines but that some twenty-six of these young people were water baptized in the prayer and praise segment after the retreat closed. Prior to the closing, on the evening preceding the day of the retreat's closing, Grace noticed that a young fellow had walked out of the meeting. She later learned that he was nineteen years old and had just come out of an insane asylum in New York. Grace said she slipped out of the meeting and sat beside him at an oak tree and "led him to the Lord."

To her surprise, the young man asked where she and Clarence lived on the campus. Grace told him that she and Clarence lived in Casselberry, Florida. The young man asked for the Casselberry address and telephone number. When Grace and Clarence returned home, their yard was covered with pup tents peopled by the twenty-seven kids who had come with their motorcoach, beat-up car, and motorcycles.

As soon as Grace and Clarence arrived, the kids were asking what literature Clarence and Grace read, what they recommended, and where to find it. There were so many kids that Grace and

Clarence called in their sponsees to take the kids through the Steps in shifts. Clarence and Grace's sponsees were taking the kids through their Steps in shifts and then to the local bookstores to search for books. Grace said the young people kept asking Grace and Clarence's babies when Grace and Clarence fought. That is what they had been used to seeing in marriages.

The young people crept to the bedroom door at night expecting to hear fights when the couple retired. Grace realized that these young people had not learned how to live without anger and hate. She said she believed the greatest reason for the success for the many that she and Clarence took through the Twelve Steps was that they could see love and service in action in the lives of Clarence and Grace together.

Dr. Bob never took Clarence through the Twelve Steps per se because the Steps had not yet been written when Clarence got sober in early 1938. However, Dr. Bob did carefully go over with Clarence the method by which Clarence was to pass on A.A.'s so-called original Six Steps which had come largely from the Oxford Group's life-changing program.

When the Big Book was published in the Spring of 1939, and Clarence had founded the first meeting of "Alcoholics Anonymous" in May of 1939, Clarence began developing specific methods for using the Good Book, the Big Book, and the Four Absolutes in taking newcomers through the Twelve Steps. But Clarence always "qualified" new people in the same way that he had qualified Grace before he would take her through the Steps.

Clarence told Grace, *"You* have to admit your alcoholism." "You have to convince *me* that you are an alcoholic. And, if necessary, I may share my experience with you so we can relate." The final qualification was embodied in this question Clarence asked Grace: He asked, "What would you do to quit drinking?" Clarence said to Grace: "The only answer I will accept is, 'I'll do anything that you say.'" Grace said to Clarence, "I thought this was a one-day-at-a-time program." Clarence replied, "It's not one day, one week, or one year. These Steps are a life-changing program, and this is the way you get your life changed. This is *forever.*" Grace said she believed Clarence's program accounted for the tremendous ninety-five percent success rate the Cleveland people achieved. They knew this was their program for the rest of their lives.

The author reviewed several materials to determine how Clarence had taken Grace and Clarence's sponsees through the Twelve Steps. The first resource was a taped address by Clarence in 1982 titled "How It Works." The second was a pamphlet titled *Going Through The Steps.* Its authorship has been attributed by a number of people to Clarence. Grace was not sure of that authorship; and Clarence's sponsee, Mitch K., recently wrote the author that he had prepared the pamphlet and submitted it to Clarence for approval. But the facts seem to be as follows.

Clarence had two sponsees named John S. and Dick S. John lived with Clarence in Florida in the early 1980's. At that time, John said to Dick S., "This stuff of Clarence's taking people through the Steps—and his other thoughts—should be put on paper. Clarence is not going to live forever." John dug out Clarence's papers and took notes as to what Clarence had written and been saying. John typed up the notes. He obtained Clarence's approval to put them in pamphlet form. Dick S. said to John, "Give me the notes, and I'll put them in two pamphlets." Dick took the notes to the printer. The printer had logos; and Dick had 500 copies each of two pamphlets printed at the same time. The first pamphlet was *My Higher Power—The Light Bulb.* And the second was *Going Through the Steps.* These two pamphlets were published for the first time, and together, in 1981 by Dick S. Reprints are currently published by Steve F. of Altamonte Springs, Florida. The author has corresponded and spoken with all three of Clarence's three sponsees (John S., Dick S., and Steve F.). Each states emphatically that the Clarence is the author of both pamphlets; that John S. gathered the material and edited it; that Clarence approved it; and that Dick S. published it. John S. told the author that Clarence had picked these three sponsees (plus Jack R.—another sponsee in Florida) to carry the message in the two pamphlets.

At any rate, Grace and Clarence's sponsees Steve and Dick do believe the pamphlet closely approximates the matters covered by Clarence in taking the Steps. Finally, the author reviewed with Grace personally her recollection of how Clarence taught her the Steps. And the following represents a presentation of Clarence's Step process, as Grace recalled it (as supplemented with the other materials just mentioned). We will set forth in order below each of the Twelve Steps. Each particular Step will be followed by Clarence's and/or Grace's comments pertaining to that Step.

Step 1

"We admitted we were powerless over alcohol—that our lives had become unmanageable."

Clarence said the First Step was intellectual. You make a decision in your *mind*. You decide that you are an alcoholic. Clarence often said, "Alcohol is mentioned only once in the Twelve Steps. Anyone can quit drinking. You need to get drink consciousness out of your mind. It takes an instructor to tell us what those Steps are going to do to us and for us. If you don't know that, you can't have a changed life. Steps One through Nine enable you to find out how to get your life on track. You have to hire a new 'Manager.'" Your own life—managed by *you*—has become unmanageable. Thus the Oxford Group, the Reverend Sam Shoemaker, and Anne Smith had all employed a prayer symbolizing what had to be done. The prayer said, "O God, manage me because I cannot manage myself." (For documentation, see Dick B., *Anne Smith's Journal*, p. 20; *Design for Living*, pp. 77, 79, 182-83; *New Light on Alcoholism*, pp. 145, 230, 300; *The Good Book and the Big Book*, p. 128.)

Step 2

"Came to believe that a Power greater than ourselves could restore us to sanity."

Clarence said to many people, "Do you want to know how I came
to believe? They told me this Power would help. I *wanted* to
believe. That's how I came to believe. I had to meet that Power in
the Third Step. The Second Step involved a step of eighteen inches
from the head to the heart—a step in which you prepare your
hearts for God."

Step 3

"Made a decision to turn our will and our lives over to the care of
God *as we understood Him.*"

As Clarence wrote in his pamphlet *My Higher Power—The
Lightbulb*, he had heard many say that the "Higher Power" could
be the Group, a piano, or a lightbulb. Clarence told Grace he had
heard people say, "Take anything you want for God." But he
taught Grace, "God has a name. His name is God, and His Son is
Jesus Christ."

Clarence said you simply must make a choice in choosing God.
He said, "I would prefer to choose a *living* God, not a dead god."
Clarence would then refer to such verses as 1 Thessalonians 1:9:
"how ye turned to God from idols to serve the living and true
God." Compare Big Book, p. 28: ". . . all of us, whatever our
race, creed, or color are children of a living Creator with whom
we may form a relationship upon simple and understandable
terms."

Clarence would quote Ephesians 4:22-24 as to the Third Step
process:

> That ye put off concerning the former conversation the old man,
> which is corrupt according to deceitful lusts; and be renewed in
> the spirit of your mind; And that ye put on the new man, which
> after God is created in righteousness and true holiness.

Clarence described the Third Step as involving a *decision*—a
decision made by the mind. Clarence felt this was the "biggest"
Step. Clarence told Grace, "I always saw God as a Big Man 'in

the wild blue yonder' with a notepad writing down all the dirty things I was doing. I had no concept of God as a kind and loving Father." Clarence said that in the Third Step, he came to know God as holding him in his arms as a natural father would his child.

Step 4
"Made a searching and fearless moral inventory of ourselves."

Clarence had a very specific approach to the Fourth Step inventory. He said too many people make long lists writing down every dirty thing they have ever done. But Clarence stressed that the inventory was *moral*. He said it was neither an *immoral* nor an *amoral* inventory. His babies were to look for the *characteristics* that *caused* them to take the actions they did. He didn't agree with the many pages and reams of yellow paper people often assembled for their Fourth Step. And he presented his sponsee with a list of some twenty items. The sponsee was to check only those specific items on the list which represented his or her defects.

The sponsee was to answer, as to each of the twenty items: "In your life, since you were born, have you ever had problems with this particular item? If so, you should put a check next to that inventory item." While the author has seen several lists that have been attributed to Clarence, Grace and Clarence's sponsees Steve F. and Dale M. indicated the following "defects" represented their best recollection of those that Clarence used for the moral inventory checklist:

1. Self-pity;
2. Self-justification;
3. Egotism (self-importance);
4. Self-condemnation;
5. Dishonesty;
6. Impatience;
7. Hate;
8. Resentments;
9. False pride (phoney);

10. Jealousy;
11. Envy;
12. Laziness;
13. Procrastination;
14. Insincerity;
15. Negative thinking;
16. Vulgar-immoral thinking;
17. Criticizing;
18. Lying;
19. Fear;
20. Greed.

Clarence said that when you had found the *nature* of your defects or shortcomings, you didn't need to know the exact wrong itself. The reason is that you have, in God's work, a "tape eraser." The specifics will be erased by God, but the nature of the defects for the specific person will still be there to challenge him or her.

The quest had to be for the *nature* of defiling, defeating, evil things man had been nurturing within himself, and which needed to be purged. Clarence would quote Mark 7:18-23:

> And he saith unto them, Are ye so without understanding also? Do ye not perceive, that whatsoever thing from without entereth into the man, *it* cannot defile him; Because it entereth not into his heart, but into the belly, and goeth out into the draught, purging all meats? And he said, That which cometh out of the man, that defileth the man. For from within, out of the heart of men, proceed evil thoughts, adulteries, fornications, murders, thefts, covetousness, wickedness, deceit, lasciviousness, an evil eye, blasphemy, pride, foolishness: All these evil things come from within, and defile the man.

Reinforcing this idea, Clarence quoted Galatians 5:16-26:

> *This* I say then, Walk in the Spirit, and ye shall not fulfil the lust of the flesh. For the flesh lusteth against the Spirit, and the Spirit

against the flesh: and these are contrary the one to the other: so that ye cannot do the things that ye would. But if ye be led of the Spirit, ye are not under the law. Now the works of the flesh are manifest, which are *these*: Adultery, fornication, uncleanness, lasciviousness, idolatry, witchcraft, hatred, variance, emulations, wrath, strife, seditions, heresies, envyings, murders, drunkenness, revellings, and such like: of the which I tell you before, as I have also told *you* in time past, that they which do such things shall not inherit the kingdom of God. But the fruit of the Spirit is love, joy, peace, longsuffering, gentleness, goodness, faith, meekness, temperance: against such there is no law. And they that are Christ's have crucified the flesh with the affections and lusts. If we live in the Spirit, let us also walk in the Spirit. Let us not be desirous of vain glory, provoking one another, envying one another.

Clarence taught that the foregoing constitute the *nature* of the things to be purged and erased.

Step 5
"Admitted to God, to ourselves, and to another human being the exact nature of our wrongs."

Clarence said the language of the Fifth Step shows you take it with a sponsor and with God. Clarence said, "God demands I talk with someone else. He says so in James 5:16, which we learned from the Oxford Group." [James 5:16 reads: "Confess *your* faults one to another, and pray for one another, that ye may be healed. The effectual fervent prayer of a righteous man availeth much."]

Step 6
"Were entirely ready to have God remove all these defects of character."

Of the Sixth Step, Clarence said: "You are asking which of the twenty defects you have, and therefore have to get rid of. In the

Sixth Step, you are saying, 'God can; I can't.'" He said the Sixth Step prepared you to take the Seventh Step on your knees.

Step 7
"Humbly asked Him to remove our shortcomings."

Clarence said, "You have freedom of choice. You can't change yourself. Only God can change you." Clarence insisted that the Seventh Step be taken on one's knees, not to become a doormat, but to get in the mood of humility. "You need to recognize who God is," said Clarence. Clarence told Grace the purpose of the procedure was to acknowledge the omniscience of God, his holiness, and his perfectness. Clarence believed God would remove the "character defects;" but that the Devil would put them right back in one's life. Using the language in Ephesians chapter 6, Clarence insisted that one needed to "put on the whole armor of God" to turn away "the fiery darts" of the Devil. Clarence told Grace to be bold and brave and use Satan's proper name to him. Clarence said, "He is the Adversary. He only comes to steal, to kill, and to destroy. He's never anything but an enemy."

For Clarence, the Seventh Step was where the new Manager (God) got out the tape eraser and erased. It was the Step in which there was a decision to get rid of the particular defects that were checked in the Fourth Step, confessed in the Fifth Step, and renounced in the Sixth Step. The assurance of God's help was given in the Sermon on the Mount. God *would* respond to the request for help. Clarence pointed to Matthew 7:7-11:

> Ask, and it shall be given you; seek, and ye shall find; knock, and it shall be opened unto you: For every one that seeketh findeth; and to him that knocketh, it shall be opened. Or what man is there of you, whom if his son ask bread, will he give him a stone? Or if he ask a fish, will he give him a serpent? If ye then, being evil, know how to give good gifts unto your children, how much more shall your Father which is in heaven give good things to them that ask him?

Clarence pointed to Psalm 103:10-12 to show the fullness of God's forgiveness—of God's simply "forgetting" and "erasing" the defects the Steps uncovered:

> He hath not dealt with us after our sins; nor rewarded us according to our iniquities. For as the heaven is high above the earth, *so* great is his mercy toward them that fear [respect or revere] him. As far as the east is from the west, *so* far hath he removed our transgressions from us.

From Dr. Bob and the Book of James, Clarence learned and applied the principle that the healing process should be the result of praying with *other* believers. God could and would "remove" the transgressions when believers prayed together. The authority for such prayer was found by the early AAs in their favorite book—James. James 5:13-16 says:

> Is any among you afflicted? let him pray. Is any merry? let him sing psalms. Is any sick among you? let him call for the elders of the church; and let them pray over him, anointing him with oil in the name of the Lord: And the prayer of faith shall save the sick, and the Lord shall raise him up; and if he have committed sins, they shall be forgiven him. Confess *your* faults one to another, and pray one for another, that ye may be healed. The effectual fervent prayer of a righteous man availeth much.

[If the reader consults our titles—Dick B., *Design for Living* and *Anne Smith's Journal*—he or she will see that both Oxford Group writers and Dr. Bob's wife Anne wrote about the *removal* of sins through prayer to God.]

Clarence was very insistent that it took hard work in prayer to confirm and believe God's "removal" of the character defects that were checked in the twenty-item inventory list and cast out through prayer on one's knees. Clarence urged his sponsees to study for three weeks the problems they had unearthed and then say the following prayer every day of the twenty-one days:

Dear God. Thank you for removing these defects from me.
Praise you, Lord. Thank you Jesus.

Clarence said you now had a brand new tape. The new Manager
had given you a clean tape because you asked for His help. His
words were, "And now you are cleaner than a hound's tooth."
Then came the tie to the Tenth Step where AAs are told to
continue to take *personal* inventory. Clarence never doubted that
the slate was wiped clean in the Seventh Step. But he pointed to
the fact that, though the evil has been cast out, it will return.

Shoemaker phrased it this way in the Oxford Group: The Devil
comes back along familiar paths. The drunk returns to drinking.
The sinner returns to sin because his Adversary is on the prowl.
Clarence pointed to Matthew 12:43-45 as the example:

> When the unclean spirit is gone out of a man, he walketh through
> dry places, seeking rest, and findeth none. Then he saith, I will
> return into my house from whence I came out; and when he is
> come, he findeth *it* empty, swept, and garnished. Then goeth he,
> and taketh with himself seven other spirits more wicked than
> himself, and they enter in and dwell there: and the last *state* of
> that man is worse than the first. Even so shall it be also unto this
> wicked generation.

Clarence said that, after the Seventh Step clean-out, the character
defects will come back and the effort to keep them at bay is a
lifetime task. Clarence said that we must be on the watch for their
return, as the Tenth Step suggests, "or we will be like the guy" in
the foregoing verses from Matthew 12.

Step 8
"Made a list of all persons we had harmed, and became willing to
make amends to them all."

Describing the Eighth Step list, Clarence pointed out that many
people put themselves at the top of the list and have a convenient
way of forgetting what *they* have done wrong. He insisted that

there be "add-ons" where appropriate. Wrongs to father, mother, siblings, the office, and others.

Step 9
"Made direct amends to such people wherever possible, except when to do so would injure them or others."

Clarence said you needed a real wise sponsor to take this step. As to Ninth Step amends, Clarence had an order of march. The first choice was "face-to-face." If that were not possible, the telephone was to be used. And if that were not possible, the baby was to "write the person he or she had harmed." Clarence added, "But do it!"

Step 10
"Continued to take personal inventory and when we were wrong promptly admitted it."

As to the continued personal inventory and prompt amends of Step Ten, Clarence said that prayer would bring the items to your attention. He said the Tenth Step involved a *personal*, not moral, inventory. You recognized the moral issues in Step Four. You were to keep watching for return of specifics in your Tenth Step personal inventory. You were to check actions each day. Clarence said to Grace he was not talking about, "Don't drink a day at a time, but how to *live* a day at a time. If you do something wrong, clean it up right away. God has forgiven everything we have done, but we get fouled up. And we ask His forgiveness when we do."

Again Clarence quoted Scripture. He pointed to the temptations the Devil presented to Jesus in the wilderness. In response, Jesus utilized the power of God and told the Devil to take a hike. Matthew 4:10-11 state:

> Then saith Jesus unto him, Get thee hence, Satan: for it is written, Thou shalt worship the Lord thy God, and him only

shalt thou serve. Then the devil leaveth him, and, behold, angels came and ministered to him.

Clarence said we could keep the defects away by the same power that God gave Jesus. Note that James 4:7 says:

Submit yourselves therefore to God. Resist the devil, and he will flee from you.

Step 11

"Sought through prayer and meditation to improve our conscious contact with God *as we understood Him*, praying only for a knowledge of His will for us and the power to carry that out."

Clarence made clear that the prayer and meditation in the Eleventh Step were the means by which you "build spiritual contact with God." He scoffed at the common statement among AAs that, "We don't ever pray for ourselves." He said, "How asinine can you get?" Grace pointed out that frequently their prayer lists (those of Grace and Clarence) were so long that they simply "anointed" them, laying hands on the list and saying, "Father, you know every need and have the answer to every question and request; and I know you know whatever the person on the list needs. You deal with it." Clarence said that prayer was talking to the new "Manager." The Manager would take you through anything. You needed to accept the power of God in your life. As to conscious contact, Clarence said, "God's right here and close. You can get answers. The men on the moon prayed. What do we pray for? We pray that He will show us what to do."

Step 12

"Having had a spiritual awakening as the result of these Steps, we tried to carry this message to alcoholics and to practice these principles in all our affairs."

Grace pointed to what she and the author agreed were the *three* parts of the Twelfth Step. Clarence said that the first part—the spiritual awakening which results from the previous Steps—occurs "in the Third Step where you meet God's Son." Clarence said the second part—the message which is to be carried—is the message of "love and service." Love and service were the two words Clarence said Dr. Bob had used to "wrap it [the message] up." Clarence said the third part—practicing the principles—involved practicing the principles of love and service in our business, home, family, church, and relationships, whether we deal with the gardener or the President.

Describing the necessary walk of love and service, Clarence told Grace, "We may be the only copy of the Big Book and the Good Book that some people will ever see. We are the example of what we have learned in walk and talk out of the Good Book and the Big Book. That in itself is a life-change." "My walk," he said, "is with the Lord and all I learned from Him about dealing with myself and my fellowman." Grace added that she and Clarence often agreed, "Satan doesn't come down with a red suit and tail. He usually comes as an angel of light." Clarence said, "We are just stewards. We let our Manager [God] guide us. God takes care of us because we are His children."

The A.A. Fellowship

Here we will talk primarily about the A.A. Fellowship as Clarence founded it and developed it in Cleveland, Ohio. There should be no doubt that Clarence observed, learned, and adopted vital fellowship ideas during his exposure to the alcoholic squad of the Oxford Group in Akron, his attendance at meetings of the Oxford Group at the T. Henry Williams home, and the immense spiritual tutoring he received at the hands of Anne Smith at A.A.'s birthplace at the Smith home in Akron. But Clarence had made a plain declaration at Dr. Bob's home on May 10, 1939: "We need a meeting which people can attend whether they have a religion or not." At that point, Clarence was very definitely referring to a non-Oxford Group meeting which his Roman Catholic babies could attend without excommunication by their Church.

Grace said to the author that Clarence's first wife had not been given deserved credit for the part she played in the Cleveland fellowship. She took drunks into Clarence's and her home. She served them refreshments. She became very close to Dr. Bob and Anne Smith, and also to Bill Wilson. But her former status as the head of the household led, Clarence said, to the end of their marriage. Dorothy had been a very capable manager of an employment agency. And, like so many of the wives of early AAs, Dorothy experienced the emergence of a new manager in her home; and the manager was not God. The manager was Clarence.

The telephone calls from drunks seeking help began to come in floods for Clarence; and the household manager status which Dorothy had occupied rapidly came to a close. Dorothy asked Clarence to leave; and from that point on until he married Selma, Clarence lived in a boarding house. When Bill Wilson made his frequent visits to Akron and to Cleveland, Bill began visiting Clarence at the boarding house. As a little-known aside, Dorothy died the same date that Bill Wilson died—February 14, 1971. At that time, she had seventeen years of sobriety in A.A.

A vital part of the highly-successful Cleveland recovery program was the development of full social lives for the newly-recovered men and their families. As Clarence put it to Grace, "They had to replace their drinking life with something of substance with their wives and family included." The Cleveland AAs had seven bowling leagues. They had softball teams (Clarence had played semi-pro baseball in his early years until no longer capable of doing so because of his drinking). Clevelanders had house parties along Oxford Group house party lines. And they frequently held picnics.

The procedure for inducting a newcomer was as follows, said Clarence. "You couldn't just walk into a meeting. We picked a man up. We gave him a Big Book and had him read it. Then Dorothy and I took him to three or four other homes to visit and get acquainted with husbands and wives who were living together.

We did this over a period of a month. This meant the new man didn't just walk cold into a meeting—fresh from his drinking, financial, and emotional problems."

Clarence began putting four-line ads in the *Cleveland Plain Dealer*. The text usually said, "If you have a problem with alcohol or know anyone who does, you can call Clarence S. [Clarence's full name was used, along with his address and telephone number]." Responses poured in from these ads and from other sources, and Clarence and his AAs could no longer handle the new people one on one. Clarence found a drunk who worked in a funeral home and lived in a carriage house at the rear. The man's name was Wally, the son of the owner of the funeral home. On meeting Wally at the carriage house, Clarence realized that the spacious quarters could be used to take *groups* of people through their Steps. Clarence announced to Wally, "I'm going to make you a captain in A.A." Wally accepted the "high honor."

Newcomers began coming in droves to Wally's carriage house at 7:30 p.m. Clarence would cruise the streets with a message which told the recipient that there was a meeting at Wally's at 7:30 seven nights a week, and that the person would get food and be ministered to. The message was given to people under bridges, empty homes, and wherever they could be found. If they were down and out, the message would be tucked into their sock or shirt.

Food was brought to the carriage house by wives and by the drunks themselves. Stale donuts were obtained from the Salvation Army, and the women would make a stock pot of soup and feed the newcomers. Clarence would teach the Twelve Steps orally and explain the Steps to those present; and then the new people were divided up and taken through the Steps one on one.

Finally, the newcomers were ready to be introduced to A.A. Fellowship meetings. The meetings were attended by the wives and children of the alcoholics. The wives would prepare coffee and food. They seldom took much part in the meetings themselves. The kids were placed on the floors to sleep. And the meetings consisted primarily of the sharing of experience, strength, and hope. They opened with the Serenity Prayer and closed with the Lord's Prayer. It was at these meetings that people were assigned a sponsor. Clarence felt sponsors should be "assigned" because newcomers were not properly equipped to select one for themselves.

Part 3

The Ministry of Clarence and Grace

8

Ambassadors for Christ in A.A.

The Commitment

Immediately after they were married, Grace and Clarence began a renewal ceremony. On each full moon, they would go out on their deck and renew their marriage vows. They had agreed that they each always ought to know where the other was coming from. And Grace believes that, within a week or ten days of their marriage, they made another mutual and life-long commitment. Together, they dedicated anew their lives to the Lord and to Alcoholics Anonymous—agreeing that they would bring all the addictive "kids" they could to a saving knowledge of Jesus Christ.

Clarence often said, "Freely give what you have so freely received. Anything you do in A.A., you do without pay." Clarence also said, "Since our A.A. program was based on the Word of God, God says there is no access to Him except through His Son Jesus Christ [see John 14:6]." Clarence said that was the basis for getting the kids on their knees and meeting Jesus.

Witnessing and Qualifying

In pursuance of their mission, Clarence and Grace led thousands of people on their knees through the Twelve Steps to the Lord Jesus Christ. Grace said to the author, "In my twenty-seven years

of leading kids through their Steps and to the Lord, and in
Clarence's forty-six years, we always qualified kids and found out
how they were reared. We asked them if anyone (nun, priest,
preacher, or anybody) had ever had them to get on their knees and
ask Jesus Christ to forgive them for their sins, thank Him for
dying in their stead, and ask Him to come into their heart and be
the Lord of their lives, and tell Him that they would love Him and
serve Him until they died or He took them home."

Grace said, "You made sure you covered those areas or you
opened yourself up to a flood of questions." Grace said, "I've led
Moslems, Buddhists, and Jews, but I've never had one kid walk
out on me. Clarence had only one. He spent all day and then
finally ushered that one to the door. Clarence said to him in love,
'If you ever change your mind and want what I have, here's my
card. Call me. I'm always here.'"

Before they would even begin to work with a newcomer, they
qualified that newcomer in three areas. In this respect, Grace's
recollection varied from that of one of Clarence's sponsees. For
Grace had been taught that you qualified the newcomer by making
him convince *himself* that he was an alcoholic; then convince his
sponsor that he was an alcoholic; and then express a willingness
to do "anything" to overcome his drinking problem. Clarence's
sponsee Steve F. recalled the three qualifications in a somewhat
different vein. Steve remembers Clarence's asking the following
three qualifying questions: (1) Do you think you have a drinking
problem? (2) Do you want to do anything about it? (3) What are
you willing to do about it?

And there were only three acceptable answers: "Yes, I have.
Yes, I do. I'll do anything." If asked what the expected answer
was, Grace or Clarence would reply, "Anything." The newcomer
was expected to declare, "I'm ready to do anything." And this was
based on the Big Book's statement that one was not ready to take
the Steps unless he had decided he wanted what AAs had and was
willing to go to any length to get it (Big Book, p. 58).

Also, in furtherance of their ambassadorial mission and service,
Grace and Clarence spoke and served at A.A. meetings,

conferences, churches, recovery centers, and wherever else they were asked. They did this without pay, accepting only transportation expenses such as airfares, and the food and housing that was provided.

The Spiritual Retreats

Clarence's most important ministry was begun before he married Grace. It was continued until Clarence's death. And it involved his "spiritual retreats" for A.A. people. [As we will see shortly, Grace has carried on with and expanded these retreats to this very day.]

Clarence established the first of these retreats at Brandon, Florida, at the United Methodist Church Scout Camp there. He was assisted by Annette N., Bill and Harriet D., Mary C., and Mary K. After Clarence married Grace, the Brandon retreat was moved to the United Methodist Adult Center at Leesburg, Florida. By the time of his death, Clarence had established another retreat at the Lutheran Bible Camp at Lake Wappogasset in Amery, Wisconsin. Shortly before he died, Clarence said to Grace, "Honey, will you keep the retreats going after I'm gone?" And Grace told him that she would until the Lord took her home or she died.

As we will discuss in a moment, Grace not only kept the retreats going, but very substantially expanded them in number.

She described the format of the retreats in the following general terms. The retreat opened with one or more lead speakers sharing experience, strength, and hope on Friday night. This was often followed by candlelight meetings in which Grace felt the young people were much more inspired to open up and share. In addition to meals on Saturday, the mornings consisted of two or more speakers—two alcoholics and one member of Al-Anon. After lunch, a speaker would lead many as a group through the Twelve Steps. During his lifetime, Clarence conducted the taking of the Steps.

Saturday night was the time for a keynote speaker, sometimes followed by one or two other speakers. The addresses were followed by a wiener roast and a marshmallow roast. In Florida, a church band entertained during the wiener roast. And Grace usually had a book full of appointments after the meeting was ended, at which time, over the years, she "led hundreds and hundreds to the Lord."

Clarence had always instructed Grace that when you took a person through the Steps, you took that person through all the Twelve Steps. But, as to these late Saturday night appointments and similar situations where Grace was simply seeing people for a short time, she asked the counsel of Clarence as to leading people to the Lord without doing all the Twelve Steps. Clarence had said there was absolutely no problem with that. If anybody was ready, he said, "Do it right there. They might not live to the next day."

Sunday mornings were reserved for a special segment titled "Came to Believe." At this time, a number of people were allotted five-minute opportunities to explain how they, in their particular lives, had come to believe in Jesus Christ as Lord and Savior.

When Grace first started attending retreats with Clarence, she had observed that the people who were conducting the retreats were taking people aside into their bedrooms and leading them to the Lord. Grace asked why it was being done in this way. And Clarence had replied that there might be strenuous objections from other sectors of Alcoholics Anonymous if this were done in a regular A.A. meeting. Grace then suggested to Clarence that the Word of God says that if we don't confess Jesus Christ to men, then he will not confess us to God and to the holy angels. She believed it was improper to take someone from a meeting to a room privately. Clarence said, "We'll pray about this matter." On a Wednesday morning, when he came to breakfast, he said, "I think I have the answer."

The answer was that Grace would announce just prior to the closing of the retreat on Sunday at noon that there would be a time of prayer and praise following the close of the retreat. She and

Clarence emphasized that the retreat would formally close with the completion of the noon meal.

From that time forward, at all the retreats, Grace would make the announcement that at one o'clock there would be prayer and praise, and that for anyone having needs of any kind, she and Clarence would be there and available. Often, on Sunday afternoons, people who attended these prayer and praise periods were baptized in the Holy Spirit and later in water.

"Life Lines"

Kids would often come to retreats quoting some of Clarence's best-known statements. They loved to hear them, and they loved to tell them. The author found the same to be true as to Grace. The following are some of the "life lines" which have inspired and challenged so many during the Christian ministry of Grace and Clarence.

Criticism:

Clarence said, "If you don't stand for something, you will fall for almost anything."

Relationships:

In response to the statement, "I'm in a relationship," Clarence would often reply, "God does not honor relationships. He only honors holy matrimony."

The Bible:

In response to the question, "Where did that come from in the Bible?" Clarence would reply, "Do you own a Bible?" If the person didn't, Clarence would give him or her a Bible. He would say, "That's a textbook. Not a novel. Not something to spot read here and there. It's a study. Read the Word. Get the Word in your heart. 'Thy word have I hid in mine heart that I might not sin against thee'" (Psalm 119:11).

Quiet Time:

Clarence said, "You know from experience that when you run around, are in a hurry and get busy, you need to get physically quiet so that God can speak to you, and you can hear Him. God says, 'Be still, and know that I am God'" (Psalm 46:10).

Meditation:

Clarence said, "Prayer is talking to God, and meditation is listening to God. God gave us two ears and one mouth; and that should tell us something."

Illumination:

Clarence said, "Don't ever open your Bible to read until you have first asked the Holy Spirit to illuminate what you need to know for that day." (See Ephesians 1:18: "The eyes of your understanding being enlightened; that ye may know . . .")

The Sermon on the Mount:

Clarence said, "That was where Christ taught His disciples how to live when He went back to the Father."

Textbooks:

Clarence said, "The Bible and the Big Book are textbooks. You never get finished. There is always new revelation when you ask for it."

Fear:

Clarence said, "When fear comes in, faith goes out the window" (Clarence often quoted Luke 12:32: "Fear not, little flock; for it is your Father's good pleasure to give you the kingdom.").

Faith:

Clarence said, "So then faith *cometh* by hearing, and hearing by the word of God" (See Romans 10:17). "That's why Grace and I would read the Bible aloud together, attend church, and listen to good teachings."

The Word "God":

Clarence said, "If the word 'God' will drive you out of A.A., booze will drive you back if you are fortunate enough to live that long."

Honesty:

Clarence said, "First, you have to have a willing mind. If they don't have a willing mind, you have to teach that baby how to get one. They've been hiding all their life, lying, and dodging."

Prayer Life:

Grace had a habit of praying in bed. When she married Clarence, she saw him get on his knees to pray at almost seventy years of age. She asked him why he got out of bed and on his knees. He said, "Have you ever found yourself praying in bed, and you wake up the next morning, and you find that you had fallen asleep while you were praying?" Then he asked me how I would feel if my best friend whom I had not seen for a long time came for a visit, and, while we were talking, that friend fell asleep. He said that was exactly what I had been doing to Almighty God, Holy God. Grace said, "That will wake you up! Man, I joined him on my knees, and that is still where I pray. I don't care how sick I am."

The Prayer Warrior:

When Clarence was taking newcomers through the Steps, Grace stayed in another room, praying—on her knees. She described herself as a "prayer warrior." Steve F. and Jack R. (Clarence's sponsees) remember well that Clarence took them through the Steps in two days and that he never saw Grace during the process.

The Unmanageable Life:

Clarence said, "There is only one Manager. That's God."

Sanity:

Grace wondered why God needed to restore her to sanity. She said, "I didn't think I was crazy." Clarence said, "Tell me episodes in your drinking career." Grace said, "I couldn't cut corners." Clarence said, "Do you think that was the action of a sane person?" Grace said, "He could knock you on your ears so nicely." Grace said, "I knew he had me. The answer was 'No.' I was not sane!"

The Devil:

Clarence said, "Call him who he is. 'Be sober, be vigilant; because your adversary the devil, as a roaring lion, walketh about, seeking whom he may devour'" (See 1 Peter 5:8).

The Hottentot:

"What do you do about the Hottentot who doesn't believe in God." Grace said, "The same thing I do with any color, any race, any creed. I teach them, and then I lead them through a Sinner's

Prayer. And most of them, even if they have two Ph.D.'s, have to be taught. And Clarence was so patient, and so kind, and took so much time to love that kid and teach that kid. See, kids have been wounded so badly, they don't trust anybody. But if you take the time to teach them and love them. . . . Man, you can't get rid of them. You'll have them forever."

"Recovered":

Grace said, "Clarence took me to the Foreword of the First Edition of A.A.'s Big Book as that Foreword appeared in the First Printing. Told me to read it. I not only read it then. I read it many times. It said:

> We, of Alcoholics Anonymous, are more than one hundred men and women who have recovered from a seemingly hopeless state of mind and body. To show other alcoholics *precisely how we have recovered* is the main purpose of this book.

"A doctor had promised me recovery in A.A. When I read that Foreword, I knew I could get well. If you're going to have a problem with my saying, 'I'm Grace. I'm a *recovered* alcoholic,' I can read you the word 'recovered' from every Foreword of every edition of the Big Book.' Clarence said the same thing all the years I knew him."

The Slow Recovery:

Clarence explained why he took people through the Steps in two days. He said, "In early A.A., people were coming in so fast there was no time for slow recovery and taking a long time to work the Twelve Steps." He simply asked: "How long do you want to stay sick?"

Church:

Echoing the advice that was usually given to Akron A.A.
newcomers, Clarence commonly and mildly suggested that they get
into a church—without suggesting which one. (Compare the report
Frank Amos made to John D. Rockefeller, Jr., concerning the
successes in Akron. Amos told Rockefeller, "Important, but not
vital, that he [the alcoholic] attend some religious service at least
once weekly." See *DR. BOB and the Good Oldtimers*, p. 131. And
Dr. Bob followed his own advice. Contrary to what many AAs
seem to believe today, Dr. Bob and his wife were charter members
of the Westminster United Presbyterian Church in Akron, Ohio,
from June 3, 1936, to April 3, 1942. And Dr. Bob later became
a communicant at St. Paul's Episcopal Church in Akron. See Dick
B., *Dr. Bob's Library*, pp. 2-3.)

The Spiritual Side of the Program:

Clarence was often asked, "What is your impression of the
spiritual side of the Program?" Clarence would reply, "There is no
spiritual side of the Program. It's all spiritual." [Cp. *Came to
Believe*, p. 6].

"The Dessert":

Clarence said: "A.A. is like a dessert—like a cake. We have our
Big Book, which is the cake. We have our Steps which are the
icing on the cake. Going through the Steps is like the whipping
cream. But the cherry on top is getting this living God—the
baptism of the Holy Spirit. You want *all* the goodies of A.A. The
'Prayer and Praise' portion after the retreat is where you get the
cherry on the top!" In Acts 1:8, Jesus gave as his last message:

> But ye shall receive power, after that the Holy Ghost is come
> upon you: and ye shall be witnesses unto me both in Jerusalem,

and in all Judaea, and in Samaria, and unto the uttermost part of the earth.

Grace added, "No matter what I asked Clarence about, he would give me an answer that would include a validation from the Scripture. His criterion was what the Word of God said. And I know he got that from Dr. Bob." (Compare *DR. BOB and the Good Oldtimers*, p. 144: "If someone asked [Dr. Bob] a question about the program, his usual response was: 'What does it say in the Good Book?'")

The Love Letter to the Kids

Clarence's kids would sometimes balk at reading the Bible because they thought it was dry and uninteresting. To which Clarence simply replied that they had to read the Bible if they wanted to know God better and know His will for them. He told them that the Bible was God's love letter to them. Grace said, "And I still use that today."

9

Grace Carries On

The Mantle

In 1966, Clarence founded the Life Enrichment Retreat at Brandon, Florida. Annette N. (now deceased) was his major assistant. As founder, Clarence had been known as the "shepherd." Steve and Sue F. had been helping out since 1979. Then, each day during Clarence's final days in the hospital in 1984, they came to visit him. On the night Clarence died, Steve and Sue entered Clarence's hospital room wet from the rain outdoors. Sue went to the right side of Clarence's bed and slid to her knees. Steve went to the left side of the bed where Grace was sitting. Clarence was able to talk only in a whisper. He greeted Steve and Sue by holding their hands for a minute.

Then he looked at Grace and said, "Estee." Grace said he was referring to the Estee Lauder cream Grace had always used in anointing people. Grace said she had a little container of the cream sitting on the bedside stand. She opened it and handed it to Clarence. Clarence anointed Sue and said, "I anoint you to be the next shepherdess of L. E. R. " (the name they all used to describe the Life Enrichment Retreat, which, by then, had been moved to Leesburg, Florida). Clarence then turned and anointed Grace to be the head shepherd of both retreats Clarence had established—the one meeting at Leesburg, Florida, and the one being conducted at

Amery, Wisconsin. By that time, Steve had dropped to the floor on his knees so that Clarence could reach him; and Clarence then anointed Steve to be the other shepherd of the Leesburg retreat. (For a biblical example of this kind of passing of responsibility, see 1 Kings 19:15-19 where God commanded Elijah to anoint Elisha to be prophet in Elijah's place.)

Sue stayed on her knees. Steve stood up and put his arms around Grace. And the shirts of all were wet with tears. Grace, Steve, and Sue had a brief conversation. Clarence was exhausted. Grace bent down and said, "Baby, would you like for the kids to go home;" and Clarence said, "Yes."

Clarence had been hospitalized with cancer for about three months prior to this last day's passing of the mantle. Grace had spent every evening of the three months sleeping in Clarence's hospital room. The day Clarence died, Grace had asked her friend Annette N. to be with Clarence some of the day while Grace was running errands. Annette asked Clarence if he would like her to read Scripture. And Clarence replied that he wanted to read the Twenty-Third Psalm. Annette said she and Clarence then traded off, reading alternate verses (illustrating how well Clarence knew and loved that Psalm).

In the last minutes before Clarence died, Grace was lying next to him on the hospital bed. She believed she heard someone singing "Amazing Grace." She asked Clarence if he heard music, and he replied that he did. Grace got out of the bed, went down the hall, and found a priest administering last rites to someone else while a lady was singing "Amazing Grace." The wife said to Grace that she knew who Grace was and where Clarence's room was; and she said, "We'll be right down there." Grace said she went back and told Clarence that there was a priest giving last rites to a man patient, and that they had said they would be right down to Clarence's room.

Clarence said, "Fine. Estee." When the three people came in, the priest asked Clarence what section of Scripture Clarence would like to have read to him. Grace started to say, "the Ninety-First Psalm;" and at the same time, Clarence said, "the Twenty-Third

Psalm." And Grace then said, "the Twenty-Third Psalm" in agreement with Clarence.

The priest anointed first Clarence and then Grace, and read the Twenty-Third Psalm. Then the three visitors just turned around; and the lady said to Grace, "I may not see you again here." But she pointed heavenward and said, "I'll see you there." The visitors walked out the door. In a few minutes, Clarence took a deep breath. He said, "Home . . . home. Home, home, home!"

With that, Clarence took his last breath.

Grace called for the charge nurse, and the nurse asked if Grace wanted Clarence removed. Grace said, "No." She packed her things. She called Steve, and she went home. Grace said she had seen a lot of people exit. But this was peaceful. She went home, read her Bible, said her prayers, went to bed, and slept.

Grace said to the author, "I was so grateful to God that He had given me those years with Clarence to know early A.A. history, to know the truth about A.A., and to know how Clarence had continued the Oxford Group principles with our Big Book."

The Spiritual Warrior

Grace still had a job to do. And she was an indomitable warrior.

In 1981, before Clarence died, Grace had undergone heart surgery involving five bypasses. That surgery eliminated the pain she had been going through. Grace said, "In three weeks, with my doctor's permission, I was on the road again traveling to retreats with Clarence for A.A." Clarence was invited nearly weekly to speak all over the United States. He accepted all of the invitations he could, and Grace was by his side.

One morning, about ninety days after Clarence's death, Grace related, "I got up in the morning, and I felt dizzy. But I had to get Chuppa her breakfast [Chuppa was Grace's dog]. I went to the refrigerator and had a real bad fogging-out spell and had to crawl back to the livingroom. I 'went out' then and didn't remember anything.

"Then the little Jewish girl that I had led to the Lord was shaking me. She told me she had passed my house, gone down as far as the golf club, turned her car around, and come back to my [Grace's] house. The screen was unlocked and the front door was unlocked. She said she had come in and found me on the floor and my little dog sitting on me. She called my doctor, Jim, who was one of us [AAs]. Jim then told her to call '911' and that he would meet us at the hospital.

"After my examinations had been completed, Jim told me that I was really going to have to fight for my life because my carotid arteries were ninety-three percent blocked on one side and ninety-seven percent blocked on the other. He said it would be touch and go and that I would really have to fight for my life. I said, 'Jim, I've always been a fighter. With God's help, I'll get through it.'" And she did. Grace could better have used the expression, "I'm a spiritual warrior." Like Clarence, she was very clear who her Adversary was; and one of her thoroughly-marked Bibles is titled *God's Victorious Army Bible: Spiritual Warfare Reference Edition 2.*

Grace tried to get her surgeon to do two surgeries at the same time. He told her she was crazy. So she had the two arteries separately operated upon a week apart. Grace said, "I was up walking the second day after my surgery." She said, "I think I was home in a week, because I remember I had to go back to the doctor to get the metal clamps removed." Grace said she immediately resumed going to retreats, sponsoring AAs, and speaking for A.A. wherever she was asked—just as she had done when Clarence was alive.

In 1989, Grace said, "I had shortness of breath. They did a cardiogram or whatever they do and found I had blockage. In those days, they wouldn't open your chest cavity a second time. So they decided to do an angioplasty.

"Two or three days after the operation, I was discharged. My doctor, Jim, was out of town receiving a prestigious award. The substitute doctor came to my room and said, 'You are released.' I said to him, 'I live alone. I haven't walked yet, and there is no one to come and get me or take care of me.' He just repeated I was released. It was Christmas, and he walked out of the room. I packed and called my A.A. sponsee Debbie. She came and got me and stayed with me in my house overnight, but she called my son Duke that night. Duke told her he would be there at 7:00 the next morning. And he arrived to take me to his home at Ponte Vedra Beach in Florida.

"It had snowed the previous evening. What was normally a two-and-a-half hour trip took eight hours because of continued snowing. By the time we arrived at Duke's home, I was purple. Duke's wife called '911' and took me to St. Luke's Hospital. The angioplasty had broken down, and I was flooded with blood. A page for a heart doctor went throughout the hospital.

"Dr. Peter Kuhlman answered the call at the Emergency Room. I don't know what happened after that. I was out. I was in the hospital three weeks. Duke did not want me to return to my home in Casselberry. So I made my home with Duke, his wife, and their two children at Ponte Vedra Beach from then until this day. In a short time, I resumed my A.A. work and continued what Clarence and I had been doing."

In 1993, Grace said that she had two by-passes that had become blocked. The doctors decided she needed to have emergency surgery. Grace said that as the nurses were preparing her for surgery, they "lost me on the table." Her heart quit beating. They sent for her son Duke and told him that if he wanted to see her, he must get to the Operating Room immediately.

While the nurses were prepping Grace for surgery, Grace insisted on standing up. She said she knew somebody had to get saved. There was a rush of people coming in and out. Grace said, "With a nurse holding me upright, I asked every person, 'Do you know the Lord as Savior.' One doctor came in. I asked him the same question; and he said, 'I think I do.'"

Grace told the author, "You never accept that as an answer." She said, "The doctor prayed the Sinner's Prayer with me, I led him to the Lord, and they carried me to the Operating Room on a gurney and completed my surgery."

As soon as they opened Grace up for the surgery, the doctors found that her mitral valve had gone out. She said that fact explained why her heart had previously stopped beating. So they repaired the mitral valve and then did two "piggybacks" to repair the blocked by-passes.

Grace had recovered one more time. Her doctor, Peter Kuhlman, said to Grace, "If I had more patients like you that had the stamina and guts to fight, my job would be a snap." Grace said, "Peter, I was born and raised to be a fighter—not a quitter; and the source of my strength and of my family's strength has always been God."

In less than ten days, Grace was back at home and in the saddle again.

The Retreats

As she had been ordained to do by Clarence on his deathbed, Grace continued the spiritual retreats at Leesburg and Amery. But there were to be many more. Grace said, "In establishing a retreat, I don't establish it in the flesh. When God sends a person to me to be a shepherd, that's when we establish a new retreat."

In the years between Clarence's death and 1995, Grace established eight new retreats. One is held at Silver Lake, St. Paul, Minnesota, with Al T. as shepherd. Another is held at Schooley's Mountain in Morristown, New Jersey. It started with Vicky W. as shepherdess; and she has been succeeded by John Z. Both these retreats were established about 1987. A third was established in Plymouth, England, about 1992 and is held twice a year. Paul D. is the shepherd. A fourth was established at Lancaster, California, in 1993, with Danny W. as shepherd and Denise K. as shepherdess.

Grace established four additional retreats which have, in the past few years, been terminated for various reasons. One was held twice a year at Lake Worth, Florida. Another at Santa Monica, California. Another at Las Vegas, Nevada. And the fourth in New York.

Two new retreats are now underway or in the wings. The first has scheduled its initial weekend at Jacksonville Beach, Florida, commencing June 28, 1996, with Jim and Cynthia S. as shepherd and shepherdess. A second is scheduled to open in 1996, at Tampa, Florida, with Tom and Laura W. as shepherd and shepherdess.

All of the retreats are held and publicized as "Spiritual Retreats for A.A. people." Al-Anons and any addicted people are welcome; and if there is an Al-Anon member present, an Al-Anon speaker is scheduled for Saturday morning. On Saturday afternoons, there are often three types of meetings—one for AAs on the Steps, one on relationships, and one for Al-Anon members. The Step meeting is held for those who want to go through the Steps in the same way they were taken in the early days of Alcoholics Anonymous. If there is any difference between a typical A.A. conference and Clarence and Grace's spiritual retreats, the retreats are, says Grace emphatically, "centered on God."

There are other special features which are a part of the Spiritual Retreats. The most important is the opportunity, made available throughout the retreat weekend, for salvation. Kids will come to Grace and the older ones throughout the weekend asking, "How many have come to the Lord so far?" (Clarence's sponsee John S. told the author that he has sometimes seen between fifty and seventy people saved in a weekend.)

Healing is available at all retreats. Grace often asks people who request healing, "Do you believe that Jesus heals today just as He did when He walked the earth?" If the answer is "Yes," Grace says they are prayed for.

"Prayer and Praise" sessions follow the close of each Retreat on Sunday afternoon. There are teachings on salvation. Then, on Acts chapter 1 and "baptism in the Holy Spirit," as Grace puts it. Then, an opportunity for water baptism by immersion. Finally, a qualified person often asks if anyone wishes to receive his or her prayer language. If so, Grace says, "the qualified person will pray for them, and they receive their prayer language" (i.e., they speak in tongues).

Meetings

Clarence often attended seven A.A. meetings a week. He always
focused on helping newcomers. Sometimes, in his later years,
Clarence would return home with a handful of newcomers' names
and telephone numbers. He would distribute these to his own
(Clarence's) sponsees, and then ask them to seek out and take the
newcomers through their Steps. Grace said, "That was an
assignment we got."

At seventy-eight years of age, Grace herself still regularly
attends three A.A. meetings a week. One is the "Beaches Unity
Group" held on Penman Road in Jacksonville Beach, Florida. This
is an open discussion meeting. Another is the "There Is a
Solution" Group, held at Our Lady Star of the Sea Church in
Ponte Vedra Beach, Florida; and this is a closed women's
discussion meeting.

Grace's third regular meeting has just adopted a new
name—"Big Book Bible Study Group;" and is held at Beaches
Chapel Assembly of God Church in Jacksonville Beach, Florida.
This meeting begins at 6:30 p.m. with members bringing covered
dishes. They say "grace" and eat. There is a fellowship time. And
the regular meeting opens with the Serenity Prayer and a
discussion of the Big Book or the Twelve Steps as well as the
reading of Scriptural references. The *Serenity for Every Day* New
Testament is used for Biblical study. There is a smoking break.
Members recount their blessings for the week; and Grace adds,
"no grumbling or complaints allowed." Members make a prayer
list for that week. If someone has been healed, or a situation has
changed, that fact is shared. The meeting closes with the Lord's
Prayer.

Just as Clarence did, Grace speaks at A.A. meetings, at
conferences, at spiritual retreats, at churches, and wherever asked
if she can fit the requests into her schedule.

Sponsorship and Twelfth Step Calls

Grace sponsors people all over the United States and the Caribbean Islands. At regular A.A. meetings, at conferences, and at retreats, Grace is frequently asked to be a sponsor. Until three years ago, she was accepting new sponsees. Today, however, she advises newcomers that she is not sponsoring additional people. She now advises the new person to obtain someone else as an A.A. sponsor, and she tries to recommend someone. However, she does work with many new people and their sponsors in the capacity of "a spiritual sponsor," as she puts it.

The Harvest

One could sit for days, weeks—even months, and never tire nor hear the end of Grace's talking about the babies. The babies she and Clarence sponsored, took through the Steps, and brought to the Lord. As the author heard some of Grace's stories, he thought of the following verses:

The harvest truly *is* plenteous, but the labourers *are* few;
Pray ye therefore the Lord of the harvest, that he will send forth labourers into his harvest (See Matthew 9:37-38).

The following accounts—presented in Grace's own words—call to view just a few whose lives have been touched and changed by the love and service given to them by Grace—the laborer.

Rashid:

Rashid was a Black Muslim. The group was doing the Steps in New York at a retreat. I was to learn that Rashid was a Black Muslim. When we got to the Third Step, all of us got on their knees. Rashid prayed the Sinner's Prayer with us. I watched his lips, but couldn't hear what he was saying. As I often do, I said, "If anyone does not feel he reached the throne of God, I'll stay here and do the Third Step one-on-one."

Rashid came up to me and said, "Miss Grace, I need some time with you. I'm a Black Muslim." I told him, "Fine, it isn't a big deal to me." I said to him, "Rashid, before we do the Sinner's Prayer, there is something you have to do." He said, "I'll do anything." Grace said, "You need to announce publicly that you are coming to Jesus and renounce all of your Muslim and other connections." Rashid said, "May I use your loudspeaker." I told him, "Yes;" and he renounced everything. I said, "Now you are ready to take the Third Step." He asked me if all the people that came with me could come up and lay their hands on him. He said, "I want Jesus Christ to be my Lord." I didn't have to ask him to say the Sinner's Prayer. He shouted it. We did it on our knees. When it was over, he got off his knees and said, "Jesus, Jesus, Jesus. Praise the Lord."

That young man had come out of a Christian family and turned away from the Lord. Later, when his father and mother were dying, Rashid called me on the telephone many times. He asked me to pray for them, and he prayed with me. Rashid was a highly-educated man. You can tell when you listen to his tapes. He had served in the priesthood of the Roman Catholic Church, but they threw him out when he became a Black Muslim. Now he's a leader in all the A.A. groups he attends in New York City. He talks at all my retreats. He's very much in demand as a speaker. He'll fly in to our retreats with three or four guys from New York who pay their own fares and come just to hear him. Whenever Rashid speaks, he recounts the whole story of the incident at the retreat in New York when he came to the Lord.

The Hindu:

The author asked Grace, "How do you take a Hindu through the Third Step?" Here was Grace's reply:

When I was in Mexico, I announced from the podium, "I do a Third Step. If you see me after, I'll explain the Third Step as Clarence taught me. That's where you get your life changed."

This Hindu raised his hand in the auditorium and said, "How do you take a Hindu through a Third Step?" That's when I asked him what he was doing in A.A. since his religion forbad him to drink alcohol. I told him his religion punishes people who drink alcohol. They cut their hands off. I told him that we take people through the Steps—One through Twelve—gently and lovingly. I didn't want the subject to come up that they could take only part of the Twelve Steps and skip the Third Step. They had to take them all.

The man got on his knees when we did the Third Step prayer and said all the prayers with everyone else. He didn't ask for any special help after the meeting was over. He was very happy with everything that happened to him.

The Jewish Girl:

Mitch, a Jewish boy, kept asking Clarence at a retreat to take him through the Steps. Mitch's wife had gotten him fired up. But because of the nature of the retreat, you couldn't just drop everything and take him through the Steps. Clarence kept putting him off. Finally, Mitch's wife, Morrie, came to me at three in the morning and said, "I can't take this anymore. I got to meet Jesus *now*." I got out of that bed and led her to the Lord. That was the most important thing in the world at that time. Clarence had frequently told the kids that they might not live until the next day and that the Word of God says "Now is the time!" (See 2 Corinthians 6:2).

Kermit:

Kermit had been a Green Beret officer. He had been in and out of A.A. for ten years. He had been separated from his wife seven or eight times. He came to me at a retreat. He took Dale (the retreat's shepherd) and me out to a pizza restaurant. He had many, many questions. He told me the history of his marriage with its many separations. And at that time he was separated. For about two-and-a-half hours, I taught him and answered every one of his questions from the Word. Dale had been Kermit's sponsor for some time, but he had gotten to the point that he was at a stalemate. That happens many times when you live in the same town and know both of the people. Kermit really was ambivalent about divorce. He thought he had read all he could in the Bible

about divorce. The meeting at the restaurant was the first crack
I saw.

Then Kermit came to the next retreat. He had asked Dale and
me during the six months that intervened between the first and
the second retreat to pray for the situation, and we did. And the
next time I saw him at the retreat, his wife was back with him.
She had moved back into their home.

I cannot remember getting on my knees with Kermit and
taking him to the Lord. I believe Dale did.

When the author first met Grace at the Amery, Wisconsin, retreat
in September of 1995, the author also met Kermit. In fact, the
author needed transportation to a talk he was giving at the Luther
Seminary in Minnesota. Dale asked Kermit to be the chauffeur.
The author and Kermit spent most of the day together. Kermit told
the author that he had been sober for eighteen months. He said he
had joined "Six for Christ." When asked who they were, Kermit
replied, "There were six AAs—Dale, myself, and four others.
They prayed for me, and I had an overwhelming feeling after just
a few days. The compulsion to drink left me, and I have not had
a drink since that time." Kermit has a very responsible job. He
works out regularly. He listens only to Christian radio stations at
Dale's suggestion; and he said he and his wife are getting along
very well.

Kermit and his wife came together to the retreat in September
of 1995. And Grace said, "When I saw him at that retreat, I knew
something had happened to him. He couldn't hide it." When the
retreat was over, Kermit and his wife, Dale and his wife and son,
Grace, and the author all had dinner together as Kermit's guests at
the very same pizza parlor to which Kermit had first invited Dale
and Grace.

10

The Point of It All

I probably went through at least three stages in my earliest days of sobriety in Alcoholics Anonymous.

The first stage involved the "D.T.'s," grand mal seizures, and acute withdrawal. Then there was the sheer joy of knowing that I had survived the experience of nearly dying, that I had joined a fellowship which seemed to subscribe to "God as we understood Him" (which allowed room for my beliefs), and that I had been much sustained in the recovery center which harbored me after my first few days in A.A.

The second stage marked the point where my troubles in sobriety really began. As delayed withdrawal set in, I shook. I suffered unbearable insomnia. I wet my pants in A.A. meetings. I was confused and dealing with substantial memory loss. I was frightened and depressed. I was facing life without drink or drug. And life seemed to promise despair, financial ruin, and long-term imprisonment. That is the way it happens for many of us.

The third stage of my new-found sobriety seemingly offered better prospects. I had been regularly attending A.A. meetings. I had taken seven Steps. I had been bringing hordes of newcomers to meetings with me. And I had begun studying the Bible—from the dubiously quiet surroundings of a V.A. psychiatric ward. But the fear, shame, guilt, and anxiety were still weighing me down.

Suddenly the truth of the promises of the Bible became embedded in my renewed mind. (See Romans 12:2.) I was lifted into a new sense of freedom—a deep believing that God loved me, and a strong conviction that I could and would depend upon God for deliverance, healing, forgiveness, and guidance. That my needs would be supplied. That God would be my sufficiency. And that an abundant life was both available and mine for the claiming.

From that point on, I was able to see the A.A. program of recovery in a new light. I studied the Big Book and the Twelve Steps assiduously. I realized the recovery program was grounded on a relationship with, and the power of God. I sought information daily from the Bible about God, His will, His power, His love, and His sufficiency in all situations. And I utilized the Big Book, the Twelve Steps, and the Bible to help a good many men recover and make new lives for themselves. The men ranged in age from sixteen to ninety. God, for sure, was no respecter of persons or of age.

But there was a new stage looming on the horizon. Now that my mind had begun clearing, I was *listening* to AAs talking *about* "spirituality" and *against* "religion." They were talking of a "higher power" who, they said, could be a chair, a lightbulb, the "group," the Big Dipper, a tree, a doorknob, and other bizarre things. They were disdainful of anyone's mentioning the Bible, Jesus Christ, or the gift of holy spirit. Worse, my own sponsor, with his sponsor egging him on, began confronting me with statements that people who read the Bible invariably got drunk; that it was wrong to lead others to Christ; and that there was something suspicious about the fact that a good many of the men I sponsored were studying the Bible and coming to a Bible fellowship to which I belonged. Finally, I got a new sponsor!

Yet that nonsense has never ceased—even to this day. Only recently an AA (who said he had over thirty-five years of sobriety) wrote me on the official A.A. stationary of an A.A. Intergroup Office. He said he was manager of that office. He sent a copy of his letter to A.A. General Services in New York. He said that my books on the Biblical origins of A.A. were "devious," "convoluted," and took a lot of "nerve." He admonished emphatically that I was to leave the writing of A.A. history to those who knew it. I might add he never indicated that he had *read* my books or that he was one of those who *knew* the history. He was just one very dry and very angry alcoholic—often called a "bleeding deacon" (as contrasted to an "elder statesman") in earlier A.A. parlance.

My recovery has not in the least been jeopardized by such episodes. But my ability *to help others* in A.A. was very substantially *hindered* in my earlier A.A. years because of them. Frankly, I was intimidated. And I set out over five years ago to find out—through extensive research—exactly and in detail what the spiritual roots of A.A. *were.*

I'm still engaged in that quest. But early on, I began asking the question: What is the point? Does anyone in A.A. or elsewhere care where A.A. came from spiritually? Does anyone want to know where early AAs got their information about God, His power, His will, and so on? Is there substantial historical proof available on the subject of early A.A.'s spiritual roots and successes? If so, does the history have applicability today? And is anyone still trying to make use of it?

There are instances in A.A.'s earlier years when some of A.A.'s founders were decrying the drift away from God. Dr. Bob's wife said using the word "group" instead of "Christ" was a "funk hole." Henrietta Seiberling frequently admonished A.A. co-founders Bill Wilson and Dr. Bob that belief in God and the power of God were taking second place in A.A. But after Dr. Bob died, Henrietta's alarms seemed to have little impact on most pioneers, other than Clarence.

Sam Shoemaker—the Episcopal priest whom Bill Wilson called a "co-founder" of A.A.—spoke to AAs about such problems through the medium of their monthly periodical, the *AA Grapevine.* As an invited guest, he spoke frankly to AAs about them from the platform at both the A.A. Twentieth Anniversary Convention in St. Louis, Missouri, in 1955, and the next International Convention at Long Beach, California, in 1960. He also covered the issues in many of his books. Shoemaker bemoaned the use of "absurd names for God" and "half-baked prayers." And he pointed to the futility of "self-made" religion. (See documentation and discussion in Dick B., *New Light on Alcoholism: The A.A. Legacy from Sam Shoemaker*, pp. 218-19, 303-04.)

But the question remained: Was anyone in A.A. listening? And until I met Grace S. and learned about Clarence S., I was never quite sure. Today I am.

I have discovered that Clarence never stopped talking about A.A.'s Biblical/Oxford Group roots. He passed the history on to his eager student and companion, Grace. And both of them have passed the history on to thousands in Alcoholics Anonymous. Grace is still doing that today.

I learned that many others in A.A. who possibly never heard of Clarence or Grace are today seeking out the early spiritual sources, books, practices, and history. They are forming study groups. They are collecting literature. And they are hungry for more. Now that my own history titles are reaching a good many AAs, I hear about these people from all over the United States and Canada. I hear from them almost daily by phone, fax, mail, and on the Internet.

Moreover, I have seen lessons from early A.A.'s spiritual roots applied in the lives of Clarence and Grace. I do not pretend to know much about their earlier years. But I have met those they have sponsored—people who are married and have families, are studying the Bible and relying on God, are trying to live by spiritual principles, and are using the Big Book and the Twelve Steps as their source for truth about A.A.'s recovery program and the spiritual principles they endeavor to apply in their lives.

In just a few months of exposure to the work of Clarence and Grace, I have seen much to commend the legacy these two people stewarded so carefully and passed along to others. In fact, I'm reminded of a segment of Philippians that was popular in early A.A. And it more than justifies the point of telling about "That Amazing Grace" and her work with Clarence.

Philippians 4:8 states:

Finally, brethren, whatsoever things are true, whatsoever things
are honest, whatsoever things *are* just, whatsoever things are
pure, whatsoever things *are* lovely, whatsoever things *are* of
good report; if *there be* any virtue, and if there be any praise,
think on these things.

I firmly believe from all that I have learned about Dr. Bob and
Anne Smith, and about Clarence and Grace S., that these A.A.
oldtimers endeavored with great zeal to stick to the truth, engage
in honest and just practices, focus on the pure and lovely, and
guard their tongues against the unfruitful. I believe, therefore, that
both virtue and praise should be given those early pioneers who
learned the principles from the Bible, helped embody them in the
Big Book, and tried to bring them into play in their daily lives
within and without the rooms of Alcoholics Anonymous.

Clarence deeply respected Dr. Bob and Anne for what they
thought, taught, and practiced. He never stopped extolling the
virtues of these people. And he certainly passed on to Grace and
those he helped the idea that there was great strength and success
in the principles that were developed in Akron from the Bible and
from the Oxford Group.

What is the point?

I believe there is tremendous need for relying on the power of
God in the A.A. of today. Not *a* god. Not just *any* god. Not just
the abandonment of *self* as god. But relying on *God*—the Creator
of whom the Big Book frequently spoke. The very language of
A.A.'s Eleventh Step bespeaks this idea. The Big Book frequently
talks of the necessity for establishing a relationship with God and
depending upon God for guidance and for power. Early A.A.
history shows where these ideas came from.

It is sad indeed that Twelve Step programs have come to be
characterized in bookstores, catalogues, talks, and tapes as "self-
help" programs. For it was "divine help" of which the Big Book
spoke (page 43) and *divine* help that was relied upon for the
seventy-five percent or higher success rate in early A.A.

The point is that if Twelve Step programs and others today wish to tap into the power of God; if they wish to rely on the access to God that was part of early A.A.; if they want to know how the pioneers prayed effectively; if they want to rely on a powerful and loving God as he was understood in early A.A.; and if they want to recover and change their lives through the divine help early A.A.'s utilized, they can find an example in the lives of Clarence and Grace S.

And they can learn from these reliable historical sources just where A.A.'s basic ideas originated. They can learn the facts as they existed—without compromise, editing, omission, or alteration. They can see that the focus in the lives of these two dedicated people was on service to God and to others—something the Big Book specifically declares to be the purpose of A.A.'s Twelve Steps. Something that Dr. Bob espoused when he declared the Steps "simmered to their essence" amounted quite simply to "love and service." And let there be no doubt that Dr. Bob was speaking of the love of God and fellow man and service to God and others as God had laid down the rules in the Bible.

It is my belief from examining the ministry and mission of Clarence and Grace S.—as revealed to me through the recollections and actions of that Amazing Grace herself—that Grace and Clarence can be credited with love and service to God and others of the kind referred to in 1 Corinthians 10:31-33:

> Whether therefore ye eat, or drink, or whatsoever ye do, do all to the glory of God. Give none offence, neither to the Jews, nor to the Gentiles, nor to the church of God: Even as I please all *men* in all *things*, not seeking mine own profit, but the *profit* of many, that they may be saved.

A challenge to be remembered by me and which should receive serious consideration by like-minded believers in the A.A. of today.

END

Afterword

"Clarence and Grace S." by Carol M., Amery, Wisconsin.

Those dear friends of our lives; it's not easy to start
to begin to convey their place in our hearts.

To pave the way for recovery to be,
our Clarence walked the path that it took to be free.
We smiled through our tears when we heard how he'd come
to his bottom on the waterfront of New York on the bum.
Though he'd told with a chuckle of hardship and pain,
we see he came far his recovery to gain.

Through the turns in his journey, the Lord had a plan
when Clarence asked for help, Dr. Bob was the man.
Though most apprehensive, he chose to submit.
Dr. Bob directed to God his life to commit.
To meetings called Oxford Bob pointed the way;
at the home of T. Henry Williams began a new day.
Though clad in his cast-offs, one shoe brown, one black,
he found a warm welcome and support did not lack.

Set out on recovery, to fix drunks was his aim;
he tried to bring in others 'til his message came.
That all should be welcome, and all could take part,
Clarence's group made the break and AA had its start.

As hurt people were reached and got well one by one,
AA began to move on; by those helped it was done.
Retreats were a way Clarence found to meet needs.
Through this, many changed lives were able to succeed.

From South Carolina came a lady named Grace.
Clarence danced into her life, and things came into place.
Grace was recovering in this program too;
she had found she was ill and did what she must do.
So "the world's oldest man" in AA found his wife.
She was astounded when he said that she'd share his life.
That lady, persuasive and gallant, with charm,
At Clarence's knee was willing the program to learn.
So Clarence's dear gruffness, frankness, and wit
teamed with her gentle radiance that many lives lit.

With their love for each other shared with me and you,
many came to their home and found lives that were new.
They loved their new kids; this was their reward,
to see others' recovery and new lives in the Lord.

Her warm understanding cracked many a shell,
love drawing out what we thought we never could tell.
They helped people come from wondering what they believed
to knowing what they stand for and God's power to receive.
Whom their God was is clear and AA's essence plain;
lives turned over to God could recovery attain.

When Clarence went to heaven, Grace was there with her smile,
supportive of others, for that is her style.
He lives on in her work and the lives they've helped change
not to mention God's work in retreats they've arranged.

Though her physical heart now says, "Grace please slow down,"
her heart of hearts seeks to bring others God's crown.
May she enjoy the river and relax for a while
and impart from her wisdom for many more miles.

With their presence our Father has blessed from above.
Clarence lives in our memories, and Grace has our love.

Index

115

Book of James 34, 35, 37, 41,
  73
Everything in this program came
  from (Clarence S.) 43
Faith without works is dead
  (James 2:20) 36
God is love (1 John 4:8, 16) 35
had to read, if they wanted to
  know God better 93
Love thy neighbor as thyself
  (James 2:8) 35
ought to be the main Source
  Book of all (Anne Smith) 44
present in his hospital room was
  the Holy Bible 33
principles of (Oxford Group
  principles are) 44
Thy will be done (Matthew
  6:10) 36
took their kids through the
  Twelve Steps 37
was God's love letter to them
  93
"ought to be the main Source
  Book of all." (Anne Smith)
  44
"soaked in the Bible" (Oxford
  Group founder-Frank
  Buchman) 45
"Bible Christian" (Sam
  Shoemaker) 45
Bible stories (Clarence's) 38
  Noah 38, 39
  rummy stories in the Bible 40
  The Good Samaritan 39
  The Prodigal Son 39, 40
Bible study 10, 15, 16, 35, 45,
  56, 57, 102
  How to study the Bible 10
  *Strong's Exhaustive
    Concordance of the Bible* 35
  The Living Bible Paraphrased
    10
  *Thompson's Chain Reference
    Bible* 10

vigorous Bible instruction from
  Dr. Bob's wife 26
Big Book xiii, xiv, xv, 7, 15, 24,
  29, 30, 35, 37, 44, 45, 48,
  50, 54, 58, 61, 62, 65, 67,
  68, 77, 78, 84, 88, 91, 92,
  97, 102, 108, 110-112
Born again 16, 27, 52
Brandon, Florida. *See* Retreats, the
  spiritual
Buchman, Dr. Frank N. D.
  (Oxford Group founder) 45,
  52
  "soaked in the Bible" 45

C

Came to believe. *See also*
  Retreats, the spiritual 49, 67,
  68, 86, 92
Came to know God. *See* Steps,
  Twelve; Step 3
Camp Farthest Out 16
Centered on God. *See* Retreats, the
  spiritual
Checking 58
Christian xiii, 3, 4, 16, 28, 43,
  45, 87, 104, 106
"Christian fellowship" (early
  Akron A.A.) 28
Clarence's first wife
  had not been given deserved
  credit 16, 78
Clark, Glenn 16
Cleveland xiii, 4, 7, 15, 16, 24,
  25, 26, 28, 29, 33, 62, 66,
  77, 78, 79
Cleveland recovery program, the
  highly-successful 78
Confess your faults one to another
  (James 5:16) 37, 71, 73
Confession (also one of the "five
  C's") 51, 53
Confidence (also one of the "five
  C's") 30, 53

Bible study 10, 15, 16, 35,
45, 56, 57, 102, 128
checking 58
continuance (five C's) 53
daily surrender 53
Five C's 53
guidance xv, 7, 47, 48, 54,
58, 108, 111
listening and writing down
leading thoughts 57
quiet time 16, 54, 56, 88
The Four Absolutes 54
major category #7: spiritual
experience 58
God consciousness 58
knowledge of God's will 58
major category #8: fellowship
fellowship with God 59
witness by life and word 59
twenty-eight (Dick B.) 46

P

P., Niles (A.A. staff member) 23
Personal inventory and prompt
amends. *See also* Steps,
Twelve 75
Philippians 4:8 111
Plymouth, England. *See* Retreats,
the spiritual
Practicing the principles of love.
See also Steps, Twelve 77
Prayer xiv, 5, 6, 15-17, 27, 31,
36, 44, 51, 57, 63, 64, 67,
71, 73, 75, 76, 80, 86-92,
99, 101-105
asking for guidance 7
for deliverance 7
"half-baked" 110
Prayer and praise. *See also*
Retreats, the spiritual 64, 86,
87, 92, 101
Prayer language. *See* Retreats, the
spiritual
Prayer warrior (Grace) 90

Principles
developed in Akron 111
from the Bible xv, 111
of early A.A. xiv, xv
of love and service 77
of the Bible 45
of the Big Book's program of
recovery 76
of the Oxford Group's Four
Absolutes 50
practicing the (third part of the
Twelfth Step) 77
spiritual 110
the recovery 110
Principles of the Oxford Group.
See Oxford Group principles
Procedure for inducting a
newcomer 78
Proverbs 10
Psalms 10, 41, 63, 73
Psalm 23 41, 96, 97
Psalm 46:10 56, 88
Psalm 91 40, 41, 96
Psalm 103:10-12 73
Psalm 119:11 63, 88
Put on the whole armor of God.
See also Steps, Twelve; Step
7 72

Q

Qualifying new people
"You have to admit your
alcoholism" 65
"You have to convince me that
you are an alcoholic" 65
I'll do anything that you say 65
Quiet time 16, 54, 56, 88

R

Rarely have we seen a person fail .
. . 62
"Religion" 43, 45, 49, 77, 104,
105, 108, 110

Twelve Traditions. *See* Traditions,
     Twelve
Twenty-Third Psalm. *See* Psalm 23

W

Wally's carriage house 79
We pray that He will show us what
     to do. *See also* Steps, Twelve
     76
Williams, T. Henry 16, 27, 28,
     77
  master bedroom of 27
Without pay 83, 85
Wives 30, 78, 79
Word of God (the Bible). *See also*
     Bible 11, 30, 57, 58, 63, 83,
     86, 89, 93, 105

Bibliography

Alcoholics Anonymous

Publications About

A Guide to the Twelve Steps of Alcoholics Anonymous. Akron: A.A. of Akron, n.d.

A Program for You: A Guide to the Big Book's Design for Living. Minnesota: Hazelden, 1991.

Alcoholics Anonymous. (multilith volume). New Jersey: Works Publishing Co., 1939.

Alcoholics Anonymous: An Interpretation of Our Twelve Steps. Washington, D.C.: "The Paragon" Creative Printers, 1944.

Alcoholics Anonymous: The Story of How More Than 100 Men Have Recovered from Alcoholism. New York City: Works Publishing Company, 1939.

A Manual for Alcoholics Anonymous. Akron: A.A. of Akron, n.d.

B., Dick. *Anne Smith's Journal, 1933-1939: A.A.'s Principles of Success*. San Rafael, CA: Paradise Research Publications, 1994.

———. *Design for Living: The Oxford Group's Contribution to Early A.A.* San Rafael, CA: Paradise Research Publications, 1995.

———. *Dr. Bob's Library: Books for Twelve Step Growth*. San Rafael, CA: Paradise Research Publications, 1994.

———. *New Light on Alcoholism: The A.A. Legacy from Sam Shoemaker*. Corte Madera, CA: Good Book Publishing Company, 1994.

———. *The Akron Genesis of Alcoholics Anonymous: An A.A.-Good Book Connection*. Corte Madera, CA: Good Book Publishing Company, 1994.

———. *The Books Early AAs Read for Spiritual Growth*. 2d. ed., San Rafael, CA: Paradise Research Publications, 1995.

———. *The Good Book and The Big Book: A.A.'s Roots in the Bible*. San Rafael, CA: Paradise Research Publications, 1995.

———, and Bill Pittman. *Courage to Change: The Christian Roots of the 12-Step Movement*. Grand Rapids, MI: Fleming H. Revell, 1994.

B., Jim. *Evolution of Alcoholics Anonymous*. New York: A.A. Archives.

B. Mel. *New Wine: The Spiritual Roots of the Twelve Step Miracle*. Minnesota: Hazelden, 1991.

Bishop, Charles, Jr. *The Washingtonians & Alcoholics Anonymous*. WV: The Bishop of Books, 1992.

———, and Bill Pittman. *To Be Continued . . . . . The Alcoholics Anonymous World Bibliography: 1935-1994*. Wheeling W. VA: The Bishop of Books, 1994.

Bufe, Charles. *Alcoholics Anonymous: Cult or Cure*. San Francisco: Sharp Press, 1991.

C., Stewart. *A Reference Guide to the Big Book of Alcoholics Anonymous*. Seattle: Recovery Press, 1986.

Central Bulletin, Volumes I-II. Cleveland: Central Committee, Oct. 1942-Sept. 1944.

Clapp, Charles, Jr. *Drinking's Not the Problem*. New York: Thomas Y. Crowell, 1949.

Conrad, Barnaby. *Time Is All We Have*. New York: Dell Publishing, 1986.

Darrah, Mary C. *Sister Ignatia: Angel of Alcoholics Anonymous*. Chicago: Loyola University Press, 1992.

Doyle, Paul Barton. *In Step with God*. Tennessee: New Directions, 1989.

E., Bob. *Handwritten note to Lois Wilson on pamphlet entitled "Four Absolutes."* (copy made available to the author at Founders Day Archives Room in Akron, Ohio, in June, 1991).

125

————. Letter from Bob E. to Nell Wing. Stepping Stones Archives.

First Steps: Al-Anon . . . 35 Years of Beginnings. New York: Al-Anon Family Group Headquarters, 1986.

Ford, Betty, with Chris Chase. *The Times of My Life.* New York: Harper and Row, 1978.

Ford, John C. *Depth Psychology, Morality and Alcoholism.* Massachusetts: Weston College, 1951.

Gray, Jerry. *The Third Strike.* Minnesota: Hazelden, 1949.

Hunter, Willard, with assistance from M. D. B. *A.A.'s Roots in the Oxford Group.* New York: A.A. Archives, 1988.

Kessell, Joseph. *The Road Back: A Report on Alcoholics Anonymous.* New York: Alfred A. Knopf, 1962.

Knippel, Charles T. *Samuel M. Shoemaker's Theological Influence on William G. Wilson's Twelve Step Spiritual Program of Recovery.* Ph. D. dissertation. St. Louis University, 1987.

Kurtz, Ernest. *Not-God: A History of Alcoholics Anonymous.* Exp. ed. Minnesota: Hazelden, 1991.

————. *Shame and Guilt: Characteristics of the Dependency Cycle.* Minnesota: Hazelden, 1981.

————, and Katherine Ketcham. *The Spirituality of Imperfection: Modern Wisdom from Classic Stories.* New York: Bantam Books, 1992.

McQ, Joe. *The Steps We Took.* Arkansas: August House Publishing, 1990.

Morreim, Dennis C. *Changed Lives: The Story of Alcoholics Anonymous.* Minneapolis: Augsburg Fortress, 1991.

Morse, Robert M, M.D., and Daniel K. Flavin, M.D. "The Definition of Alcoholism." *The Journal of the American Medical Association.* August 26, 1992, pp. 1012-14.

P., Wally. *But, for the Grace of God . . .: How Intergroups & Central Offices Carried the Message of Alcoholics Anonymous in the 1940s.* West Virginia: The Bishop of Books, 1995.

Peale, Norman Vincent. *The Power of Positive Thinking.* New York: Prentice-Hall, 1952.

Pittman, Bill. *AA The Way It Began.* Seattle: Glen Abbey Books, 1988.

Poe, Stephen E. and Frances E. *A Concordance to Alcoholics Anonymous.* Nevada: Purple Salamander Press, 1990.

Playfair, William L., M.D. *The Useful Lie.* Illinois: Crossway Books, 1991.

Robertson, Nan. *Getting Better Inside Alcoholics Anonymous.* New York: William Morrow & Co., 1988.

S., Clarence. *My Higher Power: The Light Bulb.* Winter Park, FL: Dick Stultz, 1981.

————. *My Higher Power: The Light Bulb.* 2d ed. Altamonte Springs, FL: Stephen Foreman, 1985.

————. *Going Through the Steps.* Winter Park, FL: Dick Stultz, 1981.

————. *Going Through the Steps.* 2d ed. Altamonte Springs, FL: Stephen Foreman, 1985.

Seiberling, John F. *Origins of Alcoholics Anonymous.* (A transcript of remarks by Henrietta B. Seiberling: transcript prepared by Congressman John F. Seiberling of a telephone conversation with his mother, Henrietta in the spring of 1971): Employee Assistance Quarterly. 1985; (1); pp. 8-12.

Sikorsky, Igor I., Jr. *AA's Godparents.* Minnesota: CompCare Publishers, 1990.

Smith, Bob and Sue Smith Windows. *Children of the Healer.* Illinois: Parkside Publishing Corporation, 1992.

Spiritual Milestones in Alcoholics Anonymous. Akron: A.A. of Akron, n.d.

Stafford, Tim. *The Hidden Gospel of the 12 Steps.* Christianity Today, July 22, 1991.

T., John. *A.A.: God's Instrument.* Reprint of speech delivered at Fourth Anniversary Meeting of the Chicago A.A. Group on October 5, 1943.

The Four Absolutes. Cleveland: Cleveland Central Committee of A.A., n. d.

Thomsen, Robert. *Bill W.* New York: Harper & Row, 1975.

Walker, Richmond. *For Drunks Only.* Minnesota: Hazelden, n.d.

————. *The 7 Points of Alcoholics Anonymous.* Seattle: Glen Abbey Books, 1989.

Wilson, Bill. *How The Big Book Was Put Together.* New York: A.A. General Services Archives, Transcript of Bill Wilson Speech delivered in Fort Worth, Texas, 1954.

————. *Bill Wilson's Original Story.* Bedford Hills, New York: Stepping Stones Archives, n.d., a manuscript whose individual lines are numbered 1 to 1180.

————. "Main Events: Alcoholics Anonymous Fact Sheet by Bill." November 1, 1954. Stepping Stones Archives. Bedford Hills, New York.

————. "The Fellowship of Alcoholics Anonymous." *Quarterly Journal of Studies on Alcohol.* Yale University, 1945, pp. 461-73.

————. *W. G. Wilson Recollections.* Bedford Hills, New York: Stepping Stones Archives, September 1, 1954 transcript of Bill's dictations to Ed B.

Wilson, Jan R., and Judith A. Wilson. *Addictionary: A Primer of Recovery Terms and Concepts from Abstinence to Withdrawal.* New York: Simon and Schuster, 1992.

Wilson, Lois. *Lois Remembers.* New York: Al-Anon Family Group Headquarters, 1987.

Windows, Sue Smith. (daughter of A.A.'s Co-Founder, Dr. Bob). Typewritten Memorandum entitled, *Henrietta and early Oxford Group Friends, by Sue Smith Windows.* Delivered to the author of this book by Sue Smith Windows at Akron, June, 1991.

Wing, Nell. *Grateful to Have Been There: My 42 Years with Bill and Lois, and the Evolution of Alcoholics Anonymous.* Illinois: Parkside Publishing Corporation, 1992.

Publications Approved by Alcoholics Anonymous

Alcoholics Anonymous. 3rd ed. New York: Alcoholics Anonymous World Services, Inc., 1976.

Alcoholics Anonymous. 1st ed. New Jersey: Works Publishing, 1939.

Alcoholics Anonymous Comes of Age. New York: Alcoholics Anonymous World Services, Inc., 1957.

As Bill Sees It: The A.A. Way of Life . . . selected writings of A.A.'s Co-Founder. New York: Alcoholics Anonymous World Services, Inc., 1967.

Best of the Grapevine. New York: The A.A. Grapevine, Inc., 1985.

Best of the Grapevine, Volume II. New York: The A.A. Grapevine, Inc., 1986.

Came to Believe. New York: Alcoholics Anonymous World Services, Inc., 1973.

Daily Reflections. New York: Alcoholics Anonymous World Services, Inc., 1991.

DR. BOB and the Good Oldtimers. New York: Alcoholics Anonymous World Services, Inc., 1980.

Members of the Clergy Ask about Alcoholics Anonymous. New York: Alcoholics Anonymous World Services, 1961, 1979-revised 1992, according to 1989 Conference Advisory Action.

Pass It On. New York: Alcoholics Anonymous World Services, Inc., 1984.

The A.A. Grapevine: "RHS"—issue dedicated to the memory of the Co-Founder of Alcoholics Anonymous, DR. BOB. New York: A.A. Grapevine, Inc., 1951.

The A.A. Service Manual. New York: Alcoholics Anonymous World Services, Inc., 1990-1991.

The Co-Founders of Alcoholics Anonymous. New York: Alcoholics Anonymous World Services, Inc., 1972.

The Language of the Heart. Bill W.'s Grapevine Writings. New York: The A.A. Grapevine, Inc., 1988.

Twelve Steps and Twelve Traditions. New York: Alcoholics Anonymous World Services, Inc., 1953.

The Bible—Versions of and Books About

Authorized King James Version. New York: Thomas Nelson, 1984.

Bullinger, Ethelbert W. *A Critical Lexicon and Concordance to the English and Greek New Testament.* Michigan: Zondervan, 1981.

Burns, Kenneth Charles. "The Rhetoric of Christology." Master's thesis, San Francisco State University, 1991.

Every Catholic's Guide to the Sacred Scriptures. Nashville: Thomas Nelson, 1990.

Harnack, Adolph. *The Expansion of Christianity in the First Three Centuries.* New York: G. P. Putnam's Sons, Volume I, 1904; Volume II, 1905.

Jukes, Andrew. *The Names of GOD in Holy Scripture.* Michigan: Kregel Publications, 1967.

Megivern, James J. *Official Catholic Teachings: Bible Interpretation.* North Carolina: McGrath Publishing Company, 1978.

Moffatt, James. *A New Translation of the Bible.* New York: Harper & Brothers, 1954.

New Bible Dictionary. 2d ed. Wheaton, Illinois: Tyndale House Publishers, 1987.

Orr, J. Edwin. *Full Surrender.* London: Marshall, Morgan & Scott, 1951.

Puskas, Charles B. *An Introduction to the New Testament.* Mass.: Hendrickson Publishers, 1989.

Revised Standard Version. New York: Thomas Nelson, 1952.

Serenity: A Companion for Twelve Step Recovery. Nashville: Thomas Nelson, 1990.

Strong, James. *The Exhaustive Concordance of the Bible.* Iowa: Riverside Book and Bible House, n.d.

The Abingdon Bible Commentary. New York: Abingdon Press, 1929.

The Companion Bible. Michigan: Zondervan Bible Publishers, 1964.

The Revised English Bible. Oxford: Oxford University Press, 1989.

Vine, W. E. *Vine's Expository Dictionary of Old and New Testament Words*. New York: Fleming H. Revell, 1981.
Young's Analytical Concordance to the Bible. New York: Thomas Nelson, 1982.
Zodhiates, Spiros. *The Hebrew-Greek Key Study Bible*. 6th ed. AMG Publishers, 1991.

Bible Devotionals

Chambers, Oswald. *My Utmost for His Highest*. London: Simpkin Marshall, Ltd., 1927.
Clark, Glenn, *I Will Lift Up Mine Eyes*. New York: Harper & Brothers, 1937.
Dunnington, Lewis L. *Handles of Power*. New York: Abingdon-Cokesbury Press, 1942.
Fosdick, Harry Emerson. *The Meaning of Prayer*. New York: Association Press, 1915.
Holm, Nora Smith. *The Runner's Bible*. New York: Houghton Mifflin Company, 1915.
Jones, E. Stanley. *Abundant Living*. New York: Abingdon-Cokesbury Press, 1942.
———. *Victorious Living*. New York: Abingdon Press, 1936.
Parham, A. Philip. *Letting God: Christian Meditations for Recovering Persons*. New York: Harper & Row, 1987.
The Upper Room: Daily Devotions for Family and Individual Use. Quarterly. 1st issue: April, May, June, 1935. Edited by Grover Carlton Emmons. Nashville: General Committee on Evangelism through the Department of Home Missions, Evangelism, Hospitals, Board of Missions, Methodist Episcopal Church, South.
The Two Listeners. *God Calling*. Edited by A. J. Russell. Australia: DAYSTAR, 1953.
Tileston, Mary W. *Daily Strength for Daily Needs*. Boston: Roberts Brothers, 1893.

Publications by or about the Oxford Group & Oxford Group People

A Day in Pennsylvania Honoring Frank Nathan Daniel Buchman in Pennsburg and Allentown. Oregon: Grosvenor Books, 1992.
Allen, Geoffrey Francis. *He That Cometh*. New York: The Macmillan Company, 1933.
Almond, Harry J. *Foundations for Faith*. 2d ed. London: Grosvenor Books, 1980.
———. *Iraqi Statesman: A Portrait of Mohammed Fadhel Jamali*. Salem, OR: Grosvenor Books, 1993.
Austin, H. W. "Bunny". *Frank Buchman As I Knew Him*. London: Grosvenor Books, 1975.
———. *Moral Re-Armament: The Battle for Peace*. London: William Heineman, 1938.
Begbie, Harold. *Life Changers*. New York: G. P. Putnam's Sons, 1927.
———. *Souls in Action*. New York: Hodder & Stoughton, 1911.
———. *Twice-Born Men*. New York: Fleming H. Revell, 1909.
Belden, David C. *The Origins and Development of the Oxford Group (Moral Re-Armament)*. D. Phil. Dissertation, Oxford University, 1976.
Belden, Kenneth D. *Is God Speaking-Are We Listening?* London: Grosvenor Books, 1987.
———. *Meeting Moral Re-Armament*. London: Grosvenor Books, 1979.
———. *Reflections on Moral Re-Armament*. London: Grosvenor Books, 1983.
———. *The Hour of the Helicopter*. Somerset, England: Linden Hall, 1992.
Bennett, John C. *Social Salvation*. New York: Charles Scribner's Sons, 1935.
Benson, Clarence Irving. *The Eight Points of the Oxford Group*. London: Humphrey Milford, Oxford University Press, 1936.
Blair, David. *For Tomorrow-Yes!* Compiled and edited from David Blair's Notebook by Jane Mullen Blair & Friends. New York: Exposition Press, 1981.
Blake, Howard C. *Way to Go: Adventures in Search of God's Will*. Burbank, CA: Pooh Stix Press, 1992.
Braden, Charles Samuel. *These Also Believe*. New York: The Macmillan Company, 1951.
Brown, Philip Marshall. *The Venture of Belief*. New York: Fleming H. Revell, 1935.
Buchman, Frank N. D. *Remaking the World*. London: Blandford Press, 1961.
———, and Sherwood Eddy. *Ten Suggestions for Personal Work* (not located).
———. *The Revolutionary Path: Moral Re-Armament in the thinking of Frank Buchman*. London: Grosvenor, 1975.
Frank Buchman-80. Compiled by His Friends. London: Blandford Press, 1958.

Bundy, David D. *Keswick: A Bibliographic Introduction to the Higher Life Movements*. Wilmore, Kentucky: B. L. Fisher Library of Asbury Theological Seminary, 1975.

———. "Keswick and the Experience of Evangelical Piety." Chap. 7 in *Modern Christian Revivals*. Urbana, IL: University of Illinois Press, 1992.

Campbell, Paul and Peter Howard. *Remaking Men*. New York: Arrowhead Books, 1954.

———. *The Art of Remaking Men*. Bombay: Himmat Publications, 1970.

Cantrill, Hadley. *The Psychology of Social Movements*. New York: John Wiley & Sons, Inc., 1941.

Clapp, Charles, Jr. *The Big Bender*. New York: Harper & Row, 1938.

———. *Drinking's Not the Problem*. New York: Thomas Y. Crowell, 1949.

Clark, Walter Houston. *The Oxford Group: Its History and Significance*. New York: Bookman Associates, 1951.

Cook, Sydney and Garth Lean. *The Black and White Book: A Handbook of Revolution*. London: Blandford Press, 1972.

Crossman, R. H. S. *Oxford and the Groups*. Oxford: Basil Blackwell, 1934.

Crothers, Susan. *Susan and God*. New York: Harper & Brothers, 1939.

Day, Sherwood Sunderland. *The Principles of the Group*. Oxford: University Press, n.d.

Dayton, Donald W., ed. *The Higher Christian Life: Sources for the Study of the Holiness, Pentecostal and Keswick Movements*. New York: Garland Publishing, 1984.

Dinger, Clair M. *Moral Re-Armament: A Study of Its Technical and Religious Nature in the Light of Catholic Teaching*. Washington, D.C.: The Catholic University of America Press, 1961.

"Discord in Oxford Group: Buchmanites Ousted by Disciple from N.Y. Parish House." *Newsweek*. November 24, 1941.

Dorsey, Theodore H. *From a Far Country: The Conversion Story of a Campaigner for Christ*. Huntington, Indiana: Our Sunday Visitor Press, n.d.

Driberg, Tom. *The Mystery of Moral Re-Armament: A Study of Frank Buchman and His Movement*. New York: Alfred A. Knopf, 1965.

du Maurier, Daphne. *Come Wind, Come Weather*. London: Heinemann, 1941.

Entwistle, Basil and John McCook Roots. *Moral Re-Armament: What Is It?* Pace Publications, 1967.

Eister, Allan W. *Drawing Room Conversion*. Durham: Duke University Press, 1950.

Ferguson, Charles W. *The Confusion of Tongues*. Garden City: Doubleday, Doran Company, Inc., 1940.

Foot, Stephen. *Life Began Yesterday*. New York: Harper & Brothers, 1935.

Forde, Eleanor Napier. *The Guidance of God*. London: The Oxford Group, 1927.

Gordon, Anne Wolrige. *Peter Howard, Life and Letters*. London: Hodder & Stoughton, 1969.

Gray, Betty. *Watersheds: Journey to a faith*. London: Grosvenor, 1986.

Grensted, L. W. *The Person of Christ*. New York: Harper & Brothers, 1933.

Grogan, William. *John Riffe of the Steelworkers*. New York: Coward—McCann, 1959.

Hamilton, Loudon. *MRA: How It All Began*. London: Moral Re-Armament, 1968.

Hamlin, Bryan T. *Moral Re-Armament and Forgiveness in International Affairs*. London: Grosvenor, 1992.

Harris, Irving. *An Outline of the Life of Christ*. New York: The Oxford Group, 1935.

———. *Out in Front: Forerunners of Christ. A Study of the Lives of Eight Great Men*. New York: The Calvary Evangel, 1942.

———. *The Breeze of the Spirit*. New York: The Seabury Press, 1978.

Harrison, Marjorie. *Saints Run Mad*. London: John Lane, Ltd., 1934.

Henderson, Michael. *A Different Accent*. Richmond, VA: Grosvenor Books USA, 1985.

———. *All Her Paths Are Peace: Women Pioneers in Peacemaking*. CT: Kumerian Press, 1994.

———. *Hope for a Change: Commentaries by an Optimistic Realist*. Salem, OR: Grosvenor Books, 1991.

———. *On History's Coattails: Commentaries by an English Journalist in America*. Richmond, VA: Grosvenor USA, 1988.

Henson, Herbert Hensley. *The Oxford Group Movement*. London: Oxford University Press, 1933.

Hicks, Roger. *How Augustine Found Faith: Told in his own words from F. J. Sheed's translation of The Confessions of St. Augustine*. N.p., 1956.

———. *How to Read the Bible*. London: Moral Re-Armament, 1940.

———. *Letters to Parsi*. London: Blandford Press, 1960.

———. *The Endless Adventure*. London: Blandford Press, 1964.

———. *The Lord's Prayer and Modern Man*. London: Blandford Press, 1967.

Hofmeyr, Bremer. *How to Change.* New York: Moral Re-Armament, n.d.
———. *How to Listen.* London: The Oxford Group, 1941.
Holme, Reginald. *A Journalist for God: The memoirs of Reginald Holme.* London: A Bridge Builders Publication, 1995.
Holmes-Walker, Wilfrid. *New Enlistment* (no data available).
Howard, Peter. *Frank Buchman's Secret.* Garden City: New York: Doubleday & Company, Inc., 1961.
———. *Fighters Ever.* London: Heinmann, 1941
———. *Innocent Men.* London: Heinemann, 1941.
———. *Ideas Have Legs.* London: Muller, 1945.
———. *That Man Frank Buchman.* London: Blandford Press, 1946.
———. *The World Rebuilt.* New York. Duell, Sloan & Pearce, 1951.
Hunter, T. Willard, with assistance from M.D.B. *A.A.'s Roots in the Oxford Group.* New York: A.A. Archives, 1988.
———. *Press Release.* Buchman Events/Pennsylvania, October 19, 1991.
———. *"It Started Right There" Behind the Twelve Steps and the Self-help Movement.* Oregon: Grosvenor Books, 1994.
———. *The Spirit of Charles Lindbergh: Another Dimension.* Lanham, MD: Madison Books, 1993.
———. *Uncommon Friends' Uncommon Friend.* A tribute to James Draper Newton, on the occasion of his eighty-fifth birthday. (Pamphlet, March 30, 1990).
———. *World Changing Through Life Changing.* Thesis, Newton Center, Mass: Andover-Newton Theological School, 1977.
Hutchinson, Michael. *A Christian Approach to Other Faiths.* London: Grosvenor Books, 1991.
———. *The Confessions.* (privately published study of St. Augustine's *Confessions*).
Jaeger, Clara. *Philadelphia Rebel: The Education of a Bourgeois.* Virginia: Grosvenor, 1988.
Jones, Olive M. *Inspired Children.* New York: Harper & Brothers, 1933.
———. *Inspired Youth.* New York: Harper & Brothers, 1938.
Kitchen, V. C. *I Was a Pagan.* New York: Harper & Brothers, 1934.
Koenig, His Eminence Franz Cardinal. *True Dialogue.* Oregon: Grosvenor USA, 1986.
Laun, Ferdinand. *Unter Gottes Fuhring.* The Oxford Group, n.d.
Lean, Garth. *Cast Out Your Nets.* London: Grosvenor, 1990.
———. *Frank Buchman: A Life.* London: Constable, 1985.
———. *Good God, It Works.* London: Blandford Press, 1974.
———. *On the Tail of a Comet: The Life of Frank Buchman.* Colorado Springs: Helmers & Howard, 1988.
———, and Morris Martin. *New Leadership.* London: William Heinemann, Ltd., 1936.
Leon, Philip. *The Philosophy of Courage or the Oxford Group Way.* New York: Oxford University Press, 1939.
"Less Buchmanism." *Time,* November 24, 1941.
Macintosh, Douglas C. *Personal Religion.* New York: Charles Scribner's Sons, 1942.
Mackay, Malcom George. *More than Coincidence.* Edinburgh: The Saint Andrew Press, 1979.
Macmillan, Ebenezer. *Seeking and Finding.* New York: Harper & Brothers, 1933.
Margetson, The Very Reverend Provost. *The South African Adventure.* The Oxford Group, n.d.
Martin, Morris H. *The Thunder and the Sunshine.* Washington D.C.: MRA, n.d.
———. *Born to Live in the Future.* n.l.: Up With People, 1991.
McAll, Dr. Frances. *So what's the alternative?* London: Moral Re-Armament, 1974.
Mottu, Philippe. *The Story of Caux.* London: Grosvenor, 1970.
Mowat, R. C. *Modern Prophetic Voices: From Kierkegaard to Buchman.* Oxford: New Cherwell Press, 1994.
———. *The Message of Frank Buchman.* London: Blandford Press, n.d.
———. *Report on Moral Re-Armament.* London: Blandford Press, 1955.
———. *Creating the European Community.* London, 1973.
———. *Decline and Renewal: Europe Ancient and Modern.* Oxford: New Cherwell Press, 1991.
Moyes, John S. *American Journey.* Sydney: Clarendon Publishing Co., n. d.
Murray, Robert H. *Group Movements Throughout the Ages.* New York: Harper & Brothers. 1935.
Newton, Eleanor Forde. *I Always Wanted Adventure.* London: Grosvenor, 1992.

Newton, James Draper. *Uncommon Friends: Life with Thomas Edison, Henry Ford, Harvey Firestone, Alexis Carrel, & Charles Lindbergh*. New York: Harcourt Brace, 1987.

Nichols, Beverley. *The Fool Hath Said*. Garden City: Doubleday, Doran & Company, 1936.

Orglmeister, Peter. *An Ideology for Today*. Pamphlet, 1965.

Petrocokino, Paul. *The New Man for the New World*. Cheshire: Paul Petrocokino, n.d.

———. *The Right Direction*. Great Britain: The City Press of Chester, Ltd., n.d.

———. *An Experiment: Try This for a Fortnight*. Privately published pamphlet, n.d.

Phillimore, Miles. *Just for Today*. Privately published pamphlet, 1940.

Raynor, Frank D., and Leslie D. Weatherhead. *The Finger of God*. London: Group Publications, Ltd., 1934.

Reynolds, Amelia S. *New Lives for Old*. New York. Fleming H. Revell, 1929.

Roots, John McCook. *An Apostle to Youth*. Oxford, The Oxford Group, 1928.

Rose, Cecil. *When Man Listens*. New York: Oxford University Press, 1937.

Rose, Howard J. *The Quiet Time*. New York: Oxford Group at 61 Gramercy Park, North, 1937.

Russell, Arthur J. *For Sinners Only*. London: Hodder & Stoughton, 1932.

———. *One Thing I Know*. New York: Harper & Brothers, 1933.

Sangster, W. E. *God Does Guide Us*. New York: The Abingdon Press, 1934.

Sherry, Frank H. and Mahlon H. Hellerich. *The Formative Years of Frank N. D. Buchman*. (Reprint of article at Frank Buchman home in Allentown, Pennsylvania).

Spencer, F. A. M., *The Meaning of the Groups*. London: Metheun & Co., Ltd., 1934.

Spoerri, Theophil. *Dynamic out of Silence: Frank Buchman's Relevance Today*. Translated by John Morrison. London: Grosvenor Books, 1976.

Streeter, Burnett Hillman. *The God Who Speaks*. London: Macmillan & Co., Ltd., 1936.

———. *Reality*. London, 1943.

Suenens, Rt. Rev. Msgr. *The Right View of Moral Re-Armament*. London: Burns and Oates, 1952.

The Bishop of Leicester, Chancellor R. J. Campbell and the Editor of the "Church of England Newspaper." *Stories of our Oxford House Party.*, July 17, 1931.

The Layman with a Notebook. *What Is the Oxford Group?* London: Oxford University Press, 1933.

Thornhill, Alan. *One Fight More*. London: Frederick Muller, 1943.

———. *The Significance of the Life of Frank Buchman*. London: Moral Re-Armament, 1952.

———. *Best of Friends: A Life of Enriching Friendships*. United Kingdom, Marshall Pickering, 1986.

Thornton-Duesbury, Julian P. *Sharing*. The Oxford Group. n.d.

———. *The Oxford Group: A Brief Account of its Principles and Growth*. London: The Oxford Group, 1947.

———. *The Open Secret of MRA*. London: Blandford, 1964.

———. *A Visit to Caux: First-hand experience of Moral Re-Armament in action*. London: The Oxford Group, 1960.

"Calvary's Eviction of Buchman." *Time Magazine*, November 24, 1941.

Twitchell, Kenaston. *Do You Have to Be Selfish*. New York: Moral Re-Armament, n.d.

———. *How Do You Make Up Your Mind*. New York: Moral Re-Armament, n.d.

———. *Regeneration in the Ruhr*. Princeton: Princeton University Press, 1981.

———. *Supposing Your Were Absolutely Honest*. New York: Moral Re-Armament, n.d.

———. *The Strength of a Nation: Absolute Purity*. New York: Moral Re-Armament, n.d.

Van Dusen, Henry P. "Apostle to the Twentieth Century: Frank N. D. Buchman." *Atlantic Monthly* 154 (July 1934).

———. "The Oxford Group Movement." *Atlantic Monthly*. 154 (August 1934).

Viney, Hallen. *How Do I Begin?* The Oxford Group, 61 Gramercy Park, New York., 1937.

Vrooman, Lee. *The Faith that Built America*. New York: Arrowhead Books, Inc., 1955.

Waddy, Charis. *The Skills of Discernment*. London: Grosvenor Books, 1977.

Walter, Howard A. *Soul Surgery: Some Thoughts on Incisive Personal Work*. Oxford: The Oxford Group, 1928.

Watt, Frederick B. *Great Bear: A Journey Remembered*. Yellowknife, Northwest Territories, Canada: The Northern Publishers, 1980.

Weatherhead, Leslie D. *Discipleship*. London: Student Christian Movement Press, 1934.

———. *How Can I Find God?* London: Fleming H. Revell, 1934.

————. *Psychology and Life.* New York: Abingdon Press, 1935.
West, the Right Rev. George. *The World That Works.* London: Blandford, 1945.
Williamson, Geoffrey. *Inside Buchmanism.* New York: Philosophical Library, Inc., 1955.
Winslow, Jack C. *Church in Action* (no data available to author).
————. *Vital Touch with God: How to Carry on Adequate Devotional Life.* The Evangel, 8 East 40th St., New York, n.d.
————. *When I Awake.* London: Hodder & Stoughton, 1938.
————. *Why I Believe in the Oxford Group.* London: Hodder & Stoughton, 1934.

Books by or about Oxford Group Mentors

Bushnell, Horace. *The New Life.* London: Strahan & Co., 1868.
Chapman, J. Wilbur. *Life and Work of Dwight L. Moody.* Philadelphia, 1900.
Cheney, Mary B. *Life and Letters of Horace Bushnell.* New York: Harper & Brothers, 1890.
Drummond, Henry. *Essays and Addresses.* New York: James Potts & Company, 1904.
————. *Natural Law in the Spiritual World.* Potts Edition.
————. *The Changed Life.* New York: James Potts & Company, 1891.
————. *The Greatest Thing in the World and Other Addresses.* London: Collins, 1953.
————. *The Ideal Life.* London: Hodder & Stoughton, 1897.
————. *The New Evangelism and Other Papers.* London: Hodder & Stoughton, 1899.
Edwards, Robert L. *Of Singular Genius, of Singular Grace: A Biography of Horace Bushnell.* Cleveland: The Pilgrim Press, 1992.
Findlay, James F., Jr. *Dwight L. Moody American Evangelist.* Chicago, University of Chicago Press, 1969.
Fitt, Emma Moody, *Day by Day with D. L. Moody.* Chicago: Moody Press, n.d.
Goodspeed, Edgar J. *The Wonderful Career of Moody and Sankey in Great Britain and America.* New York: Henry S. Goodspeed & Co., 1876.
Guldseth, Mark O. *Streams.* Alaska: Fritz Creek Studios, 1982.
Hopkins, C. Howard. *John R. Mott, a Biography.* Grand Rapids: William B. Erdmans Publishing Company, 1979.
James, William. *The Varieties of Religious Experience.* New York: First Vintage Books/The Library of America, 1990.
Meyer, F. B. *The Secret of Guidance.* New York: Fleming H. Revell, 1896.
Moody, Paul D. *My Father: An Intimate Portrait of Dwight Moody.* Boston: Little Brown, 1938.
Moody, William R. *The Life of D. L. Moody.* New York: Fleming H. Revell, 1900.
Mott, John R. *The Evangelization of the World in This Generation.* London, 1901.
————. *Addresses and Papers* (no further data at this time).
————. *Five Decades and a Forward View.* 4th ed. New York: Harper & Brothers, 1939.
Pollock, J. C. *Moody: A Biographical Portrait of the Pacesetter in Modern Mass Evangelism.* New York: Macmillan, 1963.
Smith, George Adam. *The Life of Henry Drummond.* New York: McClure, Phillips & Co., 1901.
Speer, Robert E. *Studies of the Man Christ Jesus.* New York: Fleming H. Revell, 1896.
————. *The Marks of a Man.* New York: Hodder & Stoughton, 1907.
————. *The Principles of Jesus.* New York: Fleming H. Revell Company, 1902.
Stewart, George, Jr. *Life of Henry B. Wright.* New York: Association Press, 1925.
Wright, Henry B. *The Will of God and a Man's Lifework.* New York: The Young Men's Christian Association Press, 1909.

Publications by or about Samuel Moor Shoemaker, Jr.

Shoemaker, Samuel Moor, Jr. "Act As If." *Christian Herald.* October, 1954.
————. "And So from My Heart I Say . . ." *The A.A. Grapevine.* New York: The A.A. Grapevine, Inc., September, 1948.
————. *. . . And Thy Neighbor.* Waco, Texas: Word Books, 1967.
————. *A Young Man's View of the Ministry.* New York: Association Press, 1923.

————. *Beginning Your Ministry.* New York: Harper & Row Publishers, 1963.
————. *By the Power of God.* New York: Harper & Brothers, 1954.
————. *Calvary Church Yesterday and Today.* New York: Fleming H. Revell, 1936.
————. *Children of the Second Birth.* New York: Fleming H. Revell, 1927.
————. *Christ and This Crisis.* New York: Fleming H. Revell, 1943.
————. *Christ's Words from the Cross.* New York: Fleming H. Revell, 1933.
————. *Confident Faith.* New York: Fleming H. Revell, 1932.
————. *Extraordinary Living for Ordinary Men.* Michigan: Zondervan, 1965.
————. *Faith at Work.* A symposium edited by Samuel Moor Shoemaker. Hawthorne Books, 1958.
————. *Freedom and Faith.* New York: Fleming H. Revell, 1949.
————. *God and America.* New York: Book Stall, 61 Gramercy Park North, New York, n.d.
————. *God's Control.* New York: Fleming H. Revell, 1939.
————. *How to Become a Christian.* New York: Harper & Brothers, 1953.
————. *How to Find God.* Reprint From Faith At Work Magazine, n.d.
————. *How to Help People.* Cincinnati: Forward Movement Publications, 1976.
————. *How You Can Find Happiness.* New York: E. P. Dutton & Co., 1947.
————. *How You Can Help Other People.* New York: E. P. Dutton & Co., 1946.
————. *If I Be Lifted Up.* New York: Fleming H. Revell, 1931.
————. *In Memoriam: The Service of Remembrance.* Princeton: The Graduate Council, Princeton University, June 10, 1956.
————. *Living Your Life Today.* New York: Fleming H. Revell, 1947.
————. "Lord, Teach Us to Pray." *Creative Help for Daily Living* (Foundation for Christian Living, Pawling, New York) 28, no. 2 (1977), Part ii.
————. *Morning Radio Talk No. 1, by Reverend Samuel M. Shoemaker,* American Broadcasting Co., 1 page transcript of program for October 4, 1945.
————. *National Awakening.* New York: Harper & Brothers, 1936.
————. *One Boy's Influence.* New York: Association Press, 1925.
————. *Realizing Religion.* New York: Association Press, 1923.
————. *Religion That Works.* New York: Fleming H. Revell, 1928.
————. *Revive Thy Church.* New York: Harper & Brothers, 1948.
————. *Sam Shoemaker at His Best.* New York: Faith At Work, 1964.
————. *So I Stand by the Door and Other Verses.* Pittsburgh: Calvary Rectory, 1958.
————. *Steps of a Modern Disciple.* Atlanta, GA: Lay Renewal Publications, 1972.
————. *The Breadth and Narrowness of the Gospel.* New York: Fleming H. Revell, 1929.
————. *The Calvary Evangel, monthly articles in.* New York. Calvary Episcopal Church.
————. *The Church Alive.* New York: E. P. Dutton & Co., Inc., 1951.
————. *The Church Can Save the World.* New York: Harper & Brothers, 1938.
————. *The Conversion of the Church.* New York: Fleming H. Revell, 1932.
————. "The Crisis of Self-Surrender." *Guideposts.* November, 1955.
————. *The Experiment of Faith.* New York: Harper & Brothers. 1957.
————. *The Gospel According to You.* New York: Fleming H. Revell, 1934.
————. *The James Houston Eccleston Day-Book: Containing a Short Account of His Life and Readings for Every Day in the Year Chosen from His Sermons.* Compiled by Samuel M. Shoemaker, Jr. New York: Longmans, Green & Co., 1915.
————. "The Spiritual Angle." *The A.A. Grapevine.* New York: The A.A. Grapevine, Inc., October, 1955.
————. *They're on the Way.* New York: E. P. Dutton, 1951.
————. "Those Twelve Steps As I Understand Them." *Best of the Grapevine: Volume II.* New York: The A.A. Grapevine, Inc., 1986.
————. *Twice-Born Ministers.* New York: Fleming H. Revell, 1929.
————. *Under New Management.* Grand Rapids: Zondervan Publishing House., 1966.
————. *What the Church Has to Learn from Alcoholics Anonymous.* Reprint of 1956 sermon. Available at A.A. Archives, New York.
————. *With the Holy Spirit and with Fire.* New York: Harper & Brothers, 1960.
————, and others. *Together.* Abingdon-Cokesbury.

A Guide to Calvary Episcopal Church: 125th Anniversary 1855-1980. Pittsburgh: Calvary Episcopal Church, 1980.

"Buchman Religion Explained to 1,000." *New York Times*. May 27, 1931.

"Campus Calls by Dr. Shoemaker Foster Chain of Religious Cells." *New York Tribune*. February 25, 1951.

Centennial History: Calvary Episcopal Church, 1855-1955. Pittsburgh: Calvary Episcopal Church, 1955.

"Church Ejects Buchman Group." *New York Times*. November 8, 1941.

"Crusaders of Reform." *Princeton Alumni Weekly*. June 2, 1993.

Cuyler, John Potter, Jr. *Calvary Church in Action*. New York: Fleming H. Revell, 1934.

Day, Sherwood S. "Always Ready: S.M.S. As a Friend." *The Evangel* (New York: Calvary Church, July-August, 1950).

Harris, Irving. *The Breeze of the Spirit*. New York: The Seabury Press, 1978.

————. "S.M.S.—Man of God for Our Time." *Faith At Work* (January-February, 1964).

"Houseparties Across the Continent." *The Christian Century*. August 23, 1933.

Knippel, Charles Taylor. *Samuel M. Shoemaker's Theological Influence on William G. Wilson's Twelve Step Spiritual Program of Recovery (Alcoholics Anonymous)*. Dissertation. St. Louis University, 1987.

"Listening to God Held Daily Need." *New York Times*. December 4, 1939.

Norton-Taylor, Duncan. "Businessmen on Their Knees." *Fortune*. October, 1953.

Olsson, Karl A. "The History of Faith at Work" (five parts). *Faith at Work News*. 1982-1983.

Peale, Norman Vincent. "The Unforgettable Sam Shoemaker." *Faith At Work*. January, 1964.

————. "The Human Touch: The Estimate of a Fellow Clergyman and Personal Friend." *The Evangel* (New York: Calvary Church, July-August, 1950).

Pitt, Louis W. "New Life, New Reality: A Brief Picture of S.M.S.'s Influence in the Diocese of New York." *Faith at Work*, July-August, 1950.

"Pittsburgh Man of the Year." *Pittsburgh Post Gazette*. January 12, 1956.

Sack, David Edward. *Sam Shoemaker and the "Happy Ethical Pagans."* Princeton, New Jersey: paper prepared in the Department of Religion, Princeton University, June, 1993.

"Sam Shoemaker and Faith at Work." Pamphlet on file at Faith At Work, Inc., 150 S. Washington St., Suite 204, Falls Church, VA 22046.

Schwartz, Robert. "Laymen and Clergy to Join Salute to Dr. S. M. Shoemaker." *Pittsburgh Press*. December 10, 1961.

Shoemaker, Helen Smith. *I Stand by the Door*. New York: Harper & Row, 1967.

"Sees Great Revival Near." *New York Times*. September 8, 1930.

Sider, Michael J. *Taking the Gospel to the Point: Evangelicals in Pittsburgh and the Origins of the Pittsburgh Leadership Foundation*. Pittsburgh: Pittsburgh Leadership Foundation, n.d.

"Soul Clinic Depicted By Pastor in Book." *New York Times*. August 5, 1927.

"Ten of the Greatest American Preachers." *Newsweek*. March 28, 1955.

The Pittsburgh Experiment's Groups. Pittsburgh: The Pittsburgh Experiment, n.d.

Tools for Christian Living. Pittsburgh: The Pittsburgh Experiment, n.d.

"Urges Church Aid Oxford Group." *New York Times*. January 2, 1933, p. 26.

Wilson, Bill. "I Stand by the Door." *The A.A. Grapevine*. New York: The A.A. Grapevine, Inc., February, 1967.

Woolverton, John F. "Evangelical Protestantism and Alcoholism 1933-1962: Episcopalian Samuel Shoemaker, The Oxford Group and Alcoholics Anonymous." *Historical Magazine of the Protestant Episcopal Church* 52 (March, 1983).

[The reader may find additional material by or about Samuel Shoemaker, Jr., at: (1) the Maryland Historical Society, Manuscripts Division, under "Shoemaker Papers;" (2) the Princeton University Archives at Princeton University, Olden Lane, Princeton, New Jersey, in the Samuel Shoemaker alumnus file; (3) the Episcopal Church Archives in Austin, Texas; (4) the Library of Congress, in the Ray Foote Purdy files of the Moral Re-Armament (and Oxford Group) Archives; (5) the Maryland Diocese of the Protestant Episcopal Church; (6) the Stepping Stones Archives, Bedford Hills, New York, the Shoemaker-Wilson letters; (7) the Hartford Theological Seminary Archives, Hartford, Connecticut; and (8) the parish offices of Calvary/St. George's in New York City. In addition, articles by or about Shoemaker were written in *The Calvary Evangel*, published by Calvary Episcopal Church in New York; in the *Faith at Work* magazine,

150 South Washington Street, Suite 204, Falls Church, Virginia; and in the literature of The Pittsburgh Experiment, 1802 Investment Building, Pittsburgh, Pennsylvania 15222.]

Spiritual Literature-Non-Oxford Group

[Almost all of these books were owned, studied, and loaned to others by Dr. Bob and his wife, Anne.]

Allen, James. *As a Man Thinketh.* New York: Peter Pauper Press, n.d.

———. *Heavenly Life.* New York: Grosset & Dunlap, n.d.

Barton, George A. *Jesus of Nazareth.* New York: The Macmillan Company, 1922.

Bode, Carl, ed. *The Portable Emerson.* New ed. New York: Penguin Books, 1981.

Brother Lawrence. *The Practice of the Presence of God.* Pennsylvania: Whitaker House, 1982.

Browne, Lewis. *This Believing World: A Simple Account of the Great Religions of Mankind.* New York: The Macmillan Co., 1935.

Carruthers, Donald W. *How to Find Reality in Your Morning Devotions.* Pennsylvania: State College, n.d.

Chambers, Oswald. *Studies in the Sermon on the Mount.* London: Simpkin, Marshall, Ltd., n.d.

Clark, Glenn. *Clear Horizons.* Vol 2. Minnesota: Macalester Park Publishing, 1941.

———. *Fishers of Men.* Boston: Little, Brown, 1928.

———. *God's Reach.* Minnesota: Macalester Park Publishing, 1951.

———. *How to Find Health through Prayer.* New York: Harper & Brothers, 1940.

———. *I Will Lift Up Mine Eyes.* New York: Harper & Brothers, 1937.

———. *Stepping Heavenward: The Spiritual Journal of Louise Miles Clark.* Minnesota: Macalester Park Publishing, 1940.

———. *The Lord's Prayer and Other Talks on Prayer from The Camps Farthest Out.* Minnesota: Macalester Publishing Co., 1932.

———. *The Man Who Talks with Flowers.* Minnesota: Macalester Park Publishing, 1939.

———. *The Soul's Sincere Desire.* Boston: Little, Brown, 1925.

———. *Touchdowns for the Lord. The Story of "Dad" A. J. Elliott.* Minnesota: Macalester Park Publishing Co., 1947.

———. *Two or Three Gathered Together.* New York: Harper & Brothers, 1942.

Daily, Starr. *Recovery.* Minnesota: Macalester Park Publishing, 1948.

Eddy, Mary Baker. *Science and Health with Key to the Scriptures.* Boston: Published by the Trustees under the Will of Mary Baker G. Eddy, 1916.

Fillmore, Charles. *Christian Healing.* Kansas City: Unity School of Christianity, 1936.

———, and Cora Fillmore. *Teach Us to Pray.* Lee's Summit, Missouri: Unity School of Christianity, 1950.

Fosdick, Harry Emerson. *A Great Time to Be Alive.* New York: Harper & Brothers, 1944.

———. *As I See Religion.* New York: Grosset & Dunlap, 1932.

———. *On Being a Real Person.* New York: Harper & Brothers, 1943.

———. *The Man from Nazareth.* New York: Harper & Brothers, 1949.

———. *The Manhood of the Master.* London: Student Christian Association, 1924.

———. *The Meaning of Faith.* New York: The Abingdon Press, 1917.

———. *The Meaning of Prayer.* New York: Association Press, 1915.

———. *The Meaning of Service.* London: Student Christian Movement, 1921.

Fox, Emmet. *Alter Your Life.* New York: Harper & Brothers, 1950.

———. *Find and Use Your Inner Power.* New York: Harper & Brothers, 1937.

———. *Power through Constructive Thinking.* New York: Harper & Brothers, 1932.

———. *Sparks of Truth.* New York: Grosset & Dunlap, 1941.

———. *The Sermon on the Mount.* New York: Harper & Row, 1934.

———. Pamphlets: *Getting Results by Prayer* (1933); *The Great Adventure* (1937); *You Must Be Born Again* (1936).

Glover, T. R. *The Jesus of History.* New York: Association Press, 1930.

Gordon, S. D. *The Quiet Time.* London: Fleming, n.d.

Heard, Gerald. *A Preface to Prayer.* New York: Harper & Brothers, 1944.

Hickson, James Moore. *Heal the Sick.* London: Methuen & Co., 1925.

James, William. *The Varieties of Religious Experience*. New York: First Vintage Press/The Library of America Edition, 1990.

Jones, E. Stanley. *Abundant Living*. New York: Cokesbury Press, 1942.

———. *Along the Indian Road*. New York: Abingdon Press, 1939.

———. *Christ and Human Suffering*. New York: Abingdon Press, 1930.

———. *Christ at the Round Table*. New York: Abingdon Press, 1928.

———. *The Choice Before Us*. New York: Abingdon Press, 1937.

———. *The Christ of Every Road*. New York: Abingdon Press, 1930.

———. *The Christ of the American Road*. New York: Abingdon-Cokesbury Press, 1944.

———. *The Christ of the Indian Road*. New York: Abingdon Press, 1925.

———. *The Christ of the Mount*. New York: Abingdon Press, 1930.

———. *Victorious Living*. New York: Abingdon Press, 1936.

———. *Way to Power and Poise*. New York: Abingdon Press, 1949.

Jung, Dr. Carl G. *Modern Man in Search of a Soul*. New York: Harcourt Brace Jovanovich, 1933.

Kagawa, Toyohiko. *Love: The Law of Life*. Philadelphia: The John C. Winston Company, 1929.

Kempis, Thomas à. *The Imitation of Christ*. Georgia: Mercer University Press, 1989.

Laubach, Frank. *Prayer (Mightiest Force in the World)*. New York: Fleming H. Revell, 1946.

Layman, Charles M. *A Primer of Prayer*. Nashville: Tidings, 1949.

Lieb, Frederick G. *Sight Unseen*. New York: Harper & Brothers, 1939.

Ligon, Ernest M. *Psychology of a Christian Personality*. New York: Macmillan, 1935.

Link, Dr. Henry C. *The Rediscovery of Man*. New York: Macmillan, 1939.

Lupton, Dilworth. *Religion Says You Can*. Boston: The Beacon Press, 1938.

Moseley, J. Rufus. *Perfect Everything*. Minnesota: Macalester Publishing Co., 1949.

Oursler, Fulton. *Happy Grotto*. Declan and McMullen, 1948.

———. *The Greatest Story Ever Told*. New York: Doubleday, 1949.

Parker, William R., and Elaine St. Johns. *Prayer Can Change Your Life*. New ed. New York: Prentice Hall, 1957.

Peale, Norman Vincent. *The Art of Living*. New York: Abingdon-Cokesbury Press, 1937.

Rawson, F. L. *The Nature of True Prayer*. Chicago: The Marlowe Company, n.d.

Sheean, Vincent. *Lead Kindly Light*. New York: Random House, 1949.

Sheen, Fulton J. *Peace of Soul*. New York: McGraw Hill, 1949.

Sheldon, Charles M. *In His Steps*. Nashville, Broadman Press, 1935.

Silkey, Charles Whitney. *Jesus and Our Generation*. Chicago: University of Chicago Press, 1925.

Speer, Robert E.. *Studies of the Man Christ Jesus*. New York: Fleming H. Revell, 1896.

Stalker, James. *The Life of Jesus Christ*. New York: Fleming H. Revell, 1891.

The Confessions of St. Augustine. Translated by E. B. Pusey. A Cardinal Edition. New York: Pocket Books, 1952.

The Fathers of the Church. New York: CIMA Publishing, 1947.

Trine, Ralph Waldo. *In Tune with the Infinite*. New York: Thomas H. Crowell, 1897.

———. *The Man Who Knew*. New York: Bobbs Merrill, 1936.

Troward, Thomas. *The Edinburgh Lectures on Mental Science*. N.p., n.d.

Uspenskii, Peter D. *Tertium Organum*. New York: A.A. Knopf, 1922.

Weatherhead, Leslie D. *Discipleship*. New York: Abingdon Press, 1934.

———. *How Can I Find God?* New York: Fleming H. Revell, 1934.

———. *Psychology and Life*. New York: Abingdon Press, 1935.

Werber, Eva Bell. *Quiet Talks with the Master*. L.A.: De Vorss & Co., 1942.

Williams, R. Llewelen, *God's Great Plan, a Guide to the Bible*. Hoverhill Destiny Publishers, n.d.

Willitts, Ethel R. *Healing in Jesus Name*. Chicago: Ethel R. Willitts Evangelists, 1931.

Dick B.'s Historical Titles on Early A.A.'s Spiritual Roots and Successes

Dr. Bob's Library: Books for Twelve Step Growth (Revised Paradise Edition)
Foreword by Ernest Kurtz, Ph.D., Author, *Not-God: A History of Alcoholics Anonymous*.
A study of the immense spiritual reading of the Bible, Christian literature, and Oxford Group books done and recommended by A.A. co-founder, Dr. Robert H. Smith. Paradise Research Pub.; 117 pp.; 6 x 9; perfect bound; 1994; $12.00; ISBN 1-885803-00-1. (Previous title: *Dr. Bob's Library: An A.A.-Good Book Connection*).

Anne Smith's Journal, 1933-1939: A.A.'s Principles of Success (Rev. Paradise Ed.)
Foreword by Robert R. Smith, son of Dr. Bob & Anne Smith; co-author, *Children of the Healer*.
Few in or out of A.A. know that Dr. Bob's wife, Anne, kept a journal in the 1930's from which shared with early AAs and their families many ideas from the Bible, the Oxford Group, and Christianity which impacted on A.A. This edition emphasizes Anne's own words. Paradise Research Publications; 176 pp.; 6 x 9; perfect bound; 1994; $14.00; ISBN 1-885803-01-X. (Previous title: *Anne Smith's Spiritual Workbook: An A.A.-Good Book Connection*).

Design for Living: The Oxford Group's Contribution to Early A.A. (Rev. Paradise Ed.)
Foreword by Rev. T. Willard Hunter; author, columnist, Oxford Group activist; former Assistant to the President of the School of Theology at Claremont, California.
A comprehensive history of the origins, principles, practices, and contributions to A.A. of "A First Century Christian Fellowship" (also known as the Oxford Group) of which A.A. was an integral part in the developmental period between 1931 and 1939. Paradise Research Publications; 432 pp.; 6 x 9; perfect bound; 1995; $17.95; ISBN 1-885803-02-8. (Previous title: *The Oxford Group & Alcoholics Anonymous: An A.A.-Good Book Connection*).

The Akron Genesis of Alcoholics Anonymous
Foreword by former U.S. Congressman John F. Seiberling, Director of the Peace Center, Akron University, whose mother, Henrietta Seiberling, was instrumental in A.A.'s founding.
The story of A.A.'s birth at Dr. Bob's Home in Akron on June 10, 1935. It tells what early AAs did in their meetings, homes, and hospital visits; what they read; and how their ideas developed from the Bible, the Oxford Group, and Christian literature. It depicts the roles of A.A. founders and their wives, and of Henrietta Seiberling, and T. Henry and Clarace Williams. Good Book Publishing; 410 pp., 6 x 9; perfect bound; 1994; $16.00; ISBN 1-881212-03-3.

The Books Early AAs Read for Spiritual Growth (Revised Paradise Edition)
An exhaustive bibliography and brief summary of all the books known to have been read and recommended for spiritual growth by early AAs in Akron and on the East Coast. Paradise Research Publications; 50 pp.; 8 1/2 x 11; spiral bound; 1995; $9.00; ISBN 1-885803-04-4.

New Light on Alcoholism: The A.A. Legacy from Sam Shoemaker
Forewords by Nickie Shoemaker Haggart, daughter of Rev. Sam Shoemaker; and Mrs. W. Irving Harris, friend of Sam Shoemaker and Bill Wilson; widow of Shoemaker's assistant minister, Rev. W. Irving Harris.
A comprehensive history and analysis of the all-but-forgotten specific contributions to A.A. spiritual principles and practices by New York's famous Episcopal preacher, the Rev. Samuel M. Shoemaker, Jr.—dubbed by Bill W. as a "co-founder" of A.A. and credited by Bill as the well-spring of A.A.'s spiritual recovery ideas. Reviews who Shoemaker was; what he said; his relationship with the Oxford Group and A.A.; and how these teachings can increase A.A.'s rate of success today. Good Book Publishing; 412 pp.; 6 x 9; perfect bound; 1994; $19.95; ISBN 1-881212-06-8.

The Good Book and The Big Book: A.A.'s Roots in the Bible
Foreword by Robert R. Smith, son of Dr. Bob & Anne Smith; co-author, *Children of the Healer*.
The author shows conclusively that A.A.'s program of recovery came primarily from the Bible. This is a history of A.A.'s biblical roots as they can be seen in A.A.'s Big Book, Twelve Steps, and Fellowship. The title will be of immense help to clergy, the recovery community, and Twelve Step adherents. Paradise Research Publications; 256 pp.; 6 x 9; perfect bound; 1995; $17.95; ISBN 1-885803-05-2.

Inquiries, orders, and requests for
catalogs and discount schedules
should be addressed to:

Dick B.
c/o Good Book Publishing Company
2747 South Kihei Road, #G-102
Kihei, Maui, Hawaii 96753
1-808-874-4876 (phone & fax)
email: 103075.767@compuserve.com
Internet Home Page: "http://www.ttx.com/dickb/"

About the Author

Dick B. writes books on the spiritual history of early A.A. They show how the basic and highly successful biblical ideas used by early AAs can be valuable tools for success in today's A.A. The religious and recovery communities are using his research and titles to work more effectively with alcoholics, addicts, and others involved in Twelve Step programs.

The author is an active, recovered member of Alcoholics Anonymous; a retired attorney; and a Bible student. He has sponsored more than sixty-five men in their recovery from alcoholism. Consistent with A.A.'s traditions of anonymity, he uses the pseudonym "Dick B."

He has had eight titles published: *The Good Book and The Big Book: A.A.'s Roots in the Bible*; *New Light on Alcoholism: The A.A. Legacy from Sam Shoemaker*; *The Books Early AAs Read for Spiritual Growth*; *Design for Living: The Oxford Group's Contribution to Early A.A.*; *The Akron Genesis of Alcoholics Anonymous*; *Anne Smith's Journal*; *Dr. Bob's Library*; and *Courage to Change* (with Bill Pittman). These have been discussed in news articles and reviewed in *Library Journal, Bookstore Journal, For A Change, The Living Church, Sober Times, NECAD Newsletter, Recovery News, Episcopal Life, MRA Newsletter*, and *Ohioana Quarterly*.

Dick is the father of two married sons (Ken and Don) and a grandfather. As a young man, he did a stint as a newspaper reporter. He attended the University of California, Berkeley, where he received his A.A. degree, majored in economics, and was elected to Phi Beta Kappa in his Junior year. In the United States Army, he was an Information-Education Specialist. He received his A.B. and J.D. degrees from Stanford University, and was Case Editor of the Stanford Law Review. Dick became interested in Bible study in his childhood Sunday School and was much inspired by his mother's almost daily study of Scripture. He joined, and later became president of, a Community Church affiliated with the United Church of Christ. By 1972, he was studying the origins of the Bible and began traveling abroad in pursuit of that subject. In 1979, he became much involved in a Biblical research, teaching, and fellowship ministry. In his community life, he was president of a merchants' council, Chamber of Commerce, church retirement center, and homeowners' association. He served on a public district board and was active in a service club.

In 1986, he was felled by alcoholism, gave up his law practice, and began recovery as a member of the Fellowship of Alcoholics Anonymous. In 1990, his interest in A.A.'s Biblical/Christian roots was sparked by his attendance at A.A.'s International Convention in Seattle. He has traveled widely; researched at archives, and at public and seminary libraries; interviewed scholars, historians, clergy, A.A. "old-timers" and survivors; and participated in programs, panels, and seminars on early A.A.'s spiritual history.

The author is the owner of Good Book Publishing Company, writes a newsletter, and has several works in progress. Much of his research and writing is done in collaboration with his older son, Ken, who holds B.A., B.Th., and M.A. degrees. Ken has been a lecturer in New Testament Greek at a Bible college and a lecturer in Fundamentals of Oral Communication at San Francisco State University. Ken is a computer specialist.

Dick is a member of the American Historical Association, the Maui Writers Guild, and The Authors' Guild. He is available for conferences, panels, seminars, and interviews.

Catalog & Order Sheet

How to Order Dick B.'s Historical Titles on Early A.A.

Order Form

Qty.

Send:

___ New Light on Alcoholism: The A.A. Legacy @ $19.95 ea. $_____
from Sam Shoemaker (Good Book Pub.)

___ The Good Book and The Big Book @ $17.95 ea. $_____
(Paradise Research Pub.)

___ Design for Living: The Oxford Group's @ $17.95 ea. $_____
Contribution to Early A.A. (Paradise Ed.)

___ That Amazing Grace: The Role of Clarence @ $16.95 ea. $_____
and Grace S. in Alcholics Anonymous
(Paradise Research Publications)

___ The Akron Genesis of Alcoholics Anonymous @ $16.00 ea. $_____
(Good Book Publishing Co.)

___ Anne Smith's Journal (Revised Paradise Ed.) @ $14.00 ea. $_____

___ Dr. Bob's Library (Revised Paradise Edition) @ $12.00 ea. $_____

___ Books Early AAs Read for Spiritual Growth @ $ 9.00 ea. $_____
(2d Edition, Paradise Research Pub.)

Shipping and Handling   Shipping and Handling $_____
Add 10% of retail price (minimum $3.00)

Total Enclosed $_____

Name: _____ (as it appears on your credit card, if using one)

Address: _____

City: _____ State: ___ Zip: _____

Tel.: _____ **Credit card**: MC VISA (please circle one) Exp. _____

CC Account #: _____ Signature _____

Special Offer for You!

A set of the author's eight titles normally sells for $123.80, plus Shipping and Handling. Using this Order Form, you may purchase **sets of eight for only $103.95 per set**, and the author will pay the Shipping and Handling for you!

Please mail this Form, with your check, money order, or credit card authorization, to: Dick B., c/o Good Book Publishing Co., 2747 S. Kihei Rd., #G-102, Kihei, HI 96753. Make your check or money order payable to "**Dick B.**" in U.S. dollars drawn on a U.S. bank. If you have any questions, please phone or fax: 1-808-874-4876.